Your
Horoscope
2022

. . . .

Cancer

22 June – 22 July

igloobooks

igloobooks

Published in 2021
First published in the UK by Igloo Books Ltd
An imprint of Igloo Books Ltd
Cottage Farm, NN6 0BJ, UK
Owned by Bonnier Books
Sveavägen 56, Stockholm, Sweden
www.igloobooks.com

0721 001
2 4 6 8 10 9 7 5 3 1
ISBN 978-1-80022-521-3

Written by Belinda Campbell and Denise Evans

Designed by Simon Parker
Edited by Natalie Graham

Printed and manufactured in China

CONTENTS
. . . .

INTRODUCTION

· · · · · · · · · · · · · · · · ·

This 15-month guide has been designed and written to give a concise and accessible insight into both the nature of your star sign and the year ahead. Divided into two main sections, the first section of this guide will give you an overview of your character in order to help you understand how you think, perceive the world and interact with others and – perhaps just as importantly – why. You'll soon see that your zodiac sign is not just affected by a few stars in the sky, but by planets, elements, and a whole host of other factors, too.

The second section of this guide is made up of daily forecasts. Use these to increase your awareness of what might appear on your horizon so that you're better equipped to deal with the days ahead. While this should never be used to dictate your life, it can be useful to see how your energies might be affected or influenced, which in turn can help you prepare for what life might throw your way.

By the end of these 15 months, these two sections should have given you a deeper understanding and awareness of yourself and, in turn, the world around you. There are never any definite certainties, but with an open mind you will find guidance for what might be, and learn to take more control of your own destiny.

THE CHARACTER
OF THE CRAB

. . . .

Cancer is the cardinal sign that kicks off summer in the zodiac calendar, and is also the first of the water signs. These summery Crabs love rounding up family and friends for a day at the beach. Creativity surrounds them, whether that means whipping up a meal for loved ones or redecorating the home. Cancerians saturate themselves with the latest trends in food, fashion, art and culture. They will have had that trendy new artist's work hanging on their walls long before anyone else can jump on the bandwagon. Or perhaps the masterpiece that Cancerians love most is their own, such as with artistic Crab Frida Kahlo. Their creative juices flow constantly and freely, and are born from a deep love and empathy.

For Cancerians, home is always where the heart is. Born in the fourth house signifying the home and family, they are best known for their unfailing love and caring nature. Some of the most beloved figures in history, such as Nelson Mandela and Diana, Princess of Wales, have been nurturing Cancerians. These homebody Crabs will usually make more of an effort than most to visit their family, wanting to surround themselves in loving and supportive atmospheres. Cancerians also love to invite people into their own home, hosting dinners, movie nights and plenty of parties – especially in their younger years. Friends and family should be careful of the crabby side, however. 'It's my party and I'll cry if I want to' probably rings true for most Cancerians. They can be overly sensitive, and are renowned for their almighty moods. Security is what they crave, and the need to settle their sometimes-unpredictable emotions.

THE CRAB

Tough on the outside yet vulnerable on the inside, the Crab symbolises many of the key traits associated with Cancerians. Those born under this sign have a negative polarity, which can mean that they are prone to processing thoughts and feelings internally, and may retreat into the safety of their own shells for long periods of time. Whilst their exterior may appear hard, Cancerians reveal their soft sensitivity to those who wait. A cosy and secure home life is an essential part of their happiness. Whether they prefer to live alone like the hermit crab or as part of a large family, Cancerians often need to spend quality time on their own for some peaceful self-reflection. With the love and support of family and friends, they can be coaxed from whatever sandy bay they may have decided to disappear into temporarily. The Crab is a unique balance of strength and vulnerability, which makes Cancerians treasured family members and fiercely reliable friends or partners.

THE MOON

The mother of the sky and the guardian sign of the zodiac calendar, the Moon and Cancerians are bonded by emotion. The Moon is the closest astronomical body to Earth, which is maybe why it feels so familiar, and why it governs homebody Cancer. There is a reassurance in being able to look up at the sky and watch the Moon's cyclical patterns, a constant quality that Cancerians are likely to find comfort in. The Moon's gravitational pull dictates Earth's tides, so any water signs will feel the influence of the Moon greatly. For Cancerians, their emotional ties to home and family are where the maternal influence of the Moon comes into effect. Cancerians are best known for their caring side, but this can turn into a worrisome nature or a tendency to smother those closest to them if they become ruled by their emotions. Both male and female Cancerians have an emotional intuition that is unparalleled, thanks to the Moon's guidance.

ELEMENTS, MODES AND POLARITIES

Each sign is made up of a unique combination of three defining groups: elements, modes and polarities. Each of these defining parts can manifest themselves in good and bad ways and none should be seen as a positive or a negative – including the polarities! Just like a jigsaw puzzle, piecing these groups together can help illuminate why each sign has certain characteristics and help us find a balance.

ELEMENTS

Fire: Dynamic and adventurous, signs with fire in them can be extroverted. Others are naturally drawn to them because of the positive light they give off, as well as their high levels of energy and confidence.

Earth: Signs with the earth element are steady and driven with their ambitions. They make for a solid friend, parent or partner due to their grounded influence and nurturing nature.

Air: The invisible element that influences each of the other elements significantly, air signs will provide much-needed perspective to others with their fair thinking, verbal skills and key ideas.

Water: Warm in the shallows and freezing as ice. This mysterious element is essential to the growth of everything around it, through its emotional depth and empathy.

MODES

Cardinal: Pioneers of the calendar, cardinal signs jump-start each season and are the energetic go-getters.

Fixed: Marking the middle of the calendar, fixed signs represent and value steadiness and reliability.

Mutable: As the seasons end, the mutable signs adapt and give themselves over gladly to the promise of change.

POLARITIES

Positive: Typically extroverted, positive signs take physical action and embrace outside stimulus in their life.

Negative: Usually introverted, negative signs value emotional development and experiencing life from the inside out.

CANCER IN BRIEF

The table below shows the key attributes of Cancerians. Use it for quick reference and to understand more about this fascinating sign.

SYMBOL	RULING PLANET	MODE	ELEMENT	HOUSE
The Crab	Moon	Cardinal	Water	Fourth

COLOUR	BODY PART	POLARITY	GENDER	POLAR SIGN
White/Silver	Breasts	Negative	Feminine	Capricorn

ROMANTIC RELATIONSHIPS

. . . .

Born in the fourth house of family and home, security can be essential to Cancerians in a relationship. Not ones for living a life made up of one-night stands, even though they might try it out in their younger years, they want to find a stable and long-term relationship. Family can be hugely important to Cancerians, so they will more often than not be asking whether they see themselves having children with potential partners on the first or second date. Whilst security is crucial, this isn't always the right approach for finding love. Allowing themselves to be vulnerable to others is an important practice for any hard-shelled Cancerians struggling to let love in.

Love is usually felt deeply and intensely by Cancerians. Being so in tune and receptive to both their own and their partner's emotions makes them some of the most intuitive lovers in the entire zodiac calendar. Cancerians often instinctively know what others need, without them having to express it. Such is their sensitivity, Cancerians will be mindful of always pleasing their lovers. This innate ability to pick up on what others want makes them hugely desirable.

Cancerians may be able to tap into emotions to form meaningful relationships, but this also has its disadvantages. They can be prone to emotional outbursts as damaging as a burst dam, or as irritating as a leaky tap. Whilst Cancerians might need to develop emotional control, an empathetic spouse who won't take their partner's outbursts to heart will help bring balance. A steady earth sign can complement water perfectly, forming a nurturing and mutually beneficial bond.

The cardinal aspect of Cancerians will usually make them happy to make the first move in love. They will also be likely to admire a fellow cardinal partner that matches their go-getter attitude.

ARIES: COMPATIBILITY 1/5

This pair shares opposite characteristics that don't always attract, sadly. A homely creature, the Cancerian may find the Arian's adventurous roaming too uncomfortable and unsettling. Conversely, the Arian will not thrive in this relationship if constricted or held back in any way by the Cancerian. However, these water and fire signs are true opposites, and therefore can stand to learn a great deal from one another. In particular, the Cancerian can teach the Arian to be more considered before acting, whilst the Arian can teach the Cancerian to be less worrisome.

TAURUS: COMPATIBILITY 5/5

Placed two positions apart on the zodiac calendar, a Cancerian and Taurean share a bond that can feel just like home. The Cancerian's frequent displays of love are deep and clear, like two names carved into a tree! The intensity of the Taurean's affection, mixed with the Cancerian's head-over-heels approach, can see these two lovers running to the altar and settling down with babies – not always in that order. Here are two signs that will do anything for each other, and will usually prefer their own little party of two.

GEMINI: COMPATIBILITY 2/5

This air and water pairing can feel too far apart personality-wise to make a good match, but the differences could actually prove to be strengthening. The Geminian is led by the mind and the Cancerian by emotion. These contrasting perspectives can lead to misunderstandings and arguments if the line of communication isn't clear. The Geminian can help the Cancerian communicate thoughts and feelings aloud rather than keeping them bottled up, while the Cancerian can provide lessons on the value of sensitivity. With so much to learn from one another, understanding and acceptance is vital to their success.

CANCER: COMPATIBILITY 4/5

The love that two Cancerians have can run as deep and mysterious as the seas from which water signs spring. The priority of creating a strong family home will be a shared goal for these two lovers, and building a large family unit will likely bring joy and satisfaction to them both. Co-parenting is something that this nurturing pair will likely excel at. With the right amount of personal space afforded to one another, these two will be able to keep their heads above water and enjoy exploring each other's depths.

LEO: COMPATIBILITY 3/5

Leo is ruled by the Sun and Cancer by the Moon, so this pairing can feel as different as night and day. However, the Lion and the Crab can also find that they have plenty in common to form a lasting love. Born in the fourth and fifth houses that partly signify family and children, the Leonian and Cancerian share a fundamental desire to find that long-term partner to settle down with. Security is essential for the Cancerian and the fixed side of the steadfast Leonian can provide just that. This power couple could go the distance if their differences are embraced.

VIRGO: COMPATIBILITY 3/5

A practical-minded Virgoan could be the balancing force that a Cancerian needs in a partner. The Virgoan will feel loved and protected by the nurturing Cancerian, but by contrast the Cancerian can at times feel hurt by the naturally critical Virgoan. Thanks to ruling planet Mercury, the Virgoan's strong communication skills should help them patch up any problems. The earth element in Virgo and the cardinal influence in Cancer can make for a driven couple, so any loving ambitions that these two share will likely be realised together.

LIBRA: COMPATIBILITY 3/5

Ruled by the planet of love and the emotions of the Moon, the romance between a Libran and Cancerian can read like an epic poem. The Libran's love for aesthetics will be particularly attractive to the creative Crab, and encourage many artistic endeavours. The home that these two could build together might well be a thing of beauty and harmony. Both cardinal characters, the Libran and Cancerian match each other's energetic attitudes, but may fight for power in the relationship. Whilst their introvert and extrovert tendencies could clash, the Libran's search for peace could help make this relationship last.

SCORPIO: COMPATIBILITY 2/5

These two water signs could easily drown in a pool of emotion. Ruled by Mars, the Scorpian's passion for the Cancerian will be intense, and the Cancerian's feelings are highly likely to be mutual. Claws and stingers at the ready, explosive disagreements could see both sides getting hurt. Both can be stubborn and unwilling to bend in an argument, which may result in them parting ways quickly. However, once these two decide that they want to be together, they can experience a love that is unfailing in its loyalty.

SAGITTARIUS: COMPATIBILITY 1/5

A Cancerian might end up feeling lost with an adventuring wanderer that is a Sagittarian. The Sagittarian can help bring out a worldlier side to the Cancerian and show that a sense of community can stretch larger than the end of the road. With the Crab, the roaming Sagittarian can learn the benefits of settling down in a loving relationship. These two have contrasting masculine and feminine energies that can complement each other greatly, if their differences are nurtured rather than discouraged. Plenty of personal time needs to be allowed to reap the many rewards from when opposites attract.

CAPRICORN: COMPATIBILITY 5/5

Opposites on the zodiac calendar, a Capricornian and Cancerian can experience a tenacious love. Symbolised often with a fish's tail, the Sea Goat that represents the Capricornian can swim happily in the Cancerian's warm waters. The Cancerian can indeed help coax a playfulness from the Capricornian that others don't always see. The Capricornian is ruled by the authoritative planet of Saturn, so could be a strong parenting partner for the family orientated Cancerian. If these two hard workers fall in love with one another, the dedication that they share could be staggering.

AQUARIUS: COMPATIBILITY 1/5

A rebellious Aquarian and security-seeking Cancerian are not always an obvious match romantically. Whilst their core character differences may be the cause of arguments, if these two can find common interests that can cement a foundation for friendship then love could still bloom. If the Cancerian can help the intellectual Aquarian to engage emotionally, then both could mutually benefit from this unlikely but special meeting of the heart and mind. Common ground to share and foreign lands to explore will be what's needed for the Aquarian and Cancerian to find a lasting love together.

PISCES: COMPATIBILITY 4/5

These two feminine and water signs can be a vision of romance together. The Cancerian recognises the changeable river of emotion that runs within Pisces, and identifies with the alternating speeds, directions and temperatures. Here are two signs that enjoy nurturing loved ones, and so their love will be built on a mutual support system. However, the Crab and Fish need to be mindful not to get swept away by the floods of emotion they are both capable of unleashing in romantic relationships. If this is kept in check, then love and compassion can flow freely.

FAMILY AND FRIENDS

. . . .

Cancerian homes are often as warm and as comforting as a cup of tea. Born into the fourth house that represents home and family, home life is of utmost importance to these expert nest-makers. Cancerians will want to make their homes an inviting environment that all the family will feel comfortable and welcome in. Capricornians make for appreciative house guests, and will be sure to notice the new artwork hanging in the artistic hallway. Cancerians who have used their creativity to decorate their own home will find that it is not wasted on aesthetic-loving Taureans, who will be full of compliments. Both Cancerians and Taureans are very much homebodies, preferring to stay in and watch a film rather than party every night, so can make highly compatible housemates.

Earth and water signs are considered to have a feminine energy and the deities associated most with the Moon are also female, so the relationships that Cancerians have with their mothers, sisters and female friends will likely help shape them greatly. The relationship with our parents plays a vital role in our overall happiness. For Cancerians, who are known for valuing family connections over most other things, this is especially applicable. Ask them to name a best friend, and they are most likely to name a parent. Cancerians likely want their own children at some stage and, if they are lucky enough to have them, will apply themselves wholeheartedly to parenting.

Cancerians are extremely intuitive beings, making them sensitive to the feelings of others. Friends and family of Cancerians might use them readily as a reliable shoulder to cry on. Cancerians are wonderful at giving loved ones reassurance and sensitive guidance, but they also expect these things in return. They can tend to dwell on the bad things that happen to them, and can hanker after constant reassurance when feeling low. When Cancerians feel like they are not receiving the sensitivity and comfort that they provide for others, they can become defensive. Retreating inwards or reacting in an overly emotional manner are both typical of Cancerians who feel like they are being attacked. Their almighty moods and grudge-holding abilities can be exhausting and alienating. Peacekeeping Libran friends could help Cancerians to balance out their emotional outbursts, whilst friendly mutable Pisceans will be able to see past the mood swings. Friends, family and Cancerians themselves will do well not to dwell too readily on disagreements and practise forgiving and forgetting. The caring gestures that Cancerians are so good at showing should hopefully remedy arguments in the long run.

MONEY AND CAREERS

. . . .

Being a particular star sign will not dictate certain types of career, but it can help identify potential areas for thriving in. Conversely, to succeed in the workplace, it is just as important to understand strengths and weaknesses to achieve career and financial goals.

For the Crab sign of the zodiac calendar, working in a social sector that helps to protect the vulnerable in society might be a natural calling. Whether it's working as police officers, firefighters or nurses, or other service roles, caring Cancerians thrive in a workplace where their protective instincts can be put to good use. Whether it is full-time work or a part-time passion, giving time to help others voluntarily can be an important part of their working life. Following in the footsteps of Cancerian philanthropist Diana, Princess of Wales, who was known for her kindness and charity, may be something that Cancerians wish to work towards.

Born in the fourth house that represents a love of home mixed with a cardinal persistence, the writing profession is well suited to Cancerians. They possess the innate ability to understand emotion, and also translate it for others. Broody Cancerians should be careful of hiding away in their writing cave for too long though, as they are known for working themselves too hard. The cardinal aspect of Cancer gives this sign the driving force to leave a lasting and positive influence on the world. Seeing their words published could be a lifelong ambition for Cancerians and they may find great success, like fellow Crab Ernest Hemingway.

· · · · · · · · · · · · · · · · · ·

As with family, colleagues cannot be chosen. Therefore, it can be advantageous to use star signs to learn about their key characteristics and discover the best ways of working together. Creative and wonderfully empathetic, two Cancerians could find sharing their artistic talents an exciting collaboration. Whilst arguments could flare up, their ability to understand one another can get them back on track to working towards a shared goal.

Sea sponges for emotions, Cancerians soak up the emotions of positive and negative people in their lives, so working with the former can be essential. Optimistic Sagittarians could be just the positive colleagues to inspire less-secure Cancerians. A lack of confidence can hold this sign back professionally, so a 'fake it until you make it' attitude could do wonders for climbing the career ladder. Deep down, Cancerians are more than capable
of rising to the top. .

The organisational skills of the Crab are well known, and this attribute means that Cancerians are likely to succeed in their chosen career, regardless of whether they are working for someone else or managing their own business.

The satisfaction of a job well done is all this sign needs to be motivated. Money itself is generally less of a motivating factor – as long as their essential needs are provided for, Cancerians are happy to sit back slightly and spend more time with the people they love, rather than clocking up the hours in the office chasing that elusive promotion or bonus. This is certainly not to say that Cancerians lack ambition or drive, simply that they can be quite happy placing their focus on the home, once their work is sorted.

HEALTH AND WELLBEING

....

Feeling things deeply, as Moon-ruled Cancerians do, means sometimes suffering from emotional insecurities and questions of self-doubt. If Cancerians find themselves sinking into anxiety, it may be that they are surrounded by too much negativity. They can be sponges for both positive and negative influences, so should review any problem areas and think how best to make improvements. A change of perspective may actually be what is required. For example, instead of wondering if they earn enough money, Cancerians should question how they can get a promotion at work. Trying to live life more fearlessly could help reduce some angst.

Spending time near water is the obvious way for Cancerians to unwind. Holidays by the coast, either home or abroad, help them to recharge their batteries and gain clarity on life. If running off to the sea isn't always feasible, taking a moment to go for a walk by a canal or pond can help them reflect on any concerns. Even a bubble bath can feel as restorative as a day at the spa.

Wellbeing practices need to be a particular priority for Cancerians. Wonderful at caring for others, they often neglect themselves. Physical exercise has been known to improve mental health and help reduce depression, and sports that lead Crabs to water, such as swimming or surfing, offer the dual benefits of both physical and emotional fitness. When exercise isn't possible, something as simple as watching a funny film could instead help lift their low moods.

Having a positive influence on the world should in turn have a positive influence on philanthropic Cancerians. Volunteering for a charity, or even setting one up, could be the legacy that they take the most joy in. They should be careful of shouldering the world's problems, however, to protect their own wellbeing. In order to truly help others, Cancerians should find and regularly practise ways of releasing worries before feeling overwhelmed. Having a place of peace and serenity in the home could help them let go of whatever stresses lay outside the front door. Weekly cleaning or decluttering sessions can also help Crabs feel more at ease.

Cancer

....

DAILY FORECASTS
for 2021

OCTOBER
. . . .

Friday 1st
In your money and value sector, the Moon asks that you
check in with your bank balance. Is it all as it should be?
An opposition to teacher Saturn may suggest that you have
stretched the budget too far. You may very well see trouble
within your relationships today.

Saturday 2nd
What's yours is yours, isn't it? You're fiercely proud of all that
you've acquired. Your social sector invites you for an evening
out, but be careful not to overdo it. Gentle persuasion or
passive-aggression will come from your love and romance
sectors today but is harmless.

Sunday 3rd
This morning the Moon dips into your communications
sector and squares off with the points of karma and fate.
What troubles you now will seem larger than it is. This is
due to Mercury connecting to Jupiter, both in retrograde,
and asking you to re-evaluate how you behave in groups
and families.

Monday 4th
Is it possible that you're not ready to begin another week? You
are drawn to being productive and getting things done but
Neptune is trying to distract you. Your dreams and plans for
future travel are on your mind. An innovative idea concerning
friendships will come to you.

Tuesday 5th

Something is asking to be changed and today you know exactly how to do it. You are methodical and practical about making a transformation of some kind. This may be your close relationships, but could also concern your finances, particularly those you share with another. Dig deep and find out.

Wednesday 6th

The planetary energy is buzzing. A new moon helps you to make new rules in your family dealings. Moon and Sun are both there with Mars making this time action-packed and assertive. The Moon then meets retrograde Mercury. On top of that, Pluto also turns direct.

Thursday 7th

Venus has had enough of seducing you and is looking for adventure in your daily duties. She also asks that you check in with your health and look after yourself better. This afternoon you can be moody and intense. Pluto needs you to make a permanent ending.

Friday 8th

Today's energy is highly charged, so be careful. The Sun is hanging around with Mars and things could get very hot. Your family sector may be extra busy or tempers may be flaring from all angles. An intense Moon sits opposite Uranus; prepare for highly volatile encounters.

Saturday 9th

Attending to mundane chores may be the best thing you can do today. Mercury meets Mars and the Sun in your family sector. Battles of ego will test your patience. Be like Mercury and say nothing. Turn your back and let them get on with it. Women will win the day.

Sunday 10th

Saturn turns direct today and reminds you that if you didn't learn a thing or two this year, it will come back around another time. An optimistic Moon connects to Saturn, Mars, Mercury and the Sun. You're emotionally charged to settle things in your family today.

Monday 11th

Work through your job list today but don't overtax yourself. Check in with your health. Your immune system may need support right now. Get that shell of yours ready for the winter. This evening your loved one is calling and a cosy night for two beckons. If single, spoil yourself.

Tuesday 12th

Business or romantic relationships demand your time and energy. Pleasant surprises or new ways of relating lift your spirits. It is possible that you see something now that was always there but out of your vision. This can excite you; you have a new toy to play with.

Wednesday 13th

The Moon meets Pluto retrograde today. This can bring unsettling feelings which you cannot pinpoint. Watch out for subtle manipulation. Your sensitive soul will perceive this as victimisation but it may be that something is changing against your will. Resistance will not get you anywhere; this needs to happen.

Thursday 14th

In your intimacy sector, the Moon meets Saturn. You will have a long discussion with an elder, or with yourself about where you have been restricted this year. The rebel inside you will surface but you manage to keep it under control. However, this will keep bubbling for a short while.

Friday 15th

Today is more optimistic. Both the Sun and Jupiter come out to play and warm your heart. You may have renewed hope in your wider groups. Jupiter is soon to go direct and you are already feeling the joy return. Emotions and ego are in sync and stable.

Saturday 16th

This weekend, your mood turns towards connecting effortlessly with others. You may find yourself engaging in spiritual activities or simply reading about them. This reignites your urge to travel and explore exotic lands. What new Holy Grail will you be chasing now? Is it the thrill of the quest that excites you?

Sunday 17th

Venus and Mercury have a talk about exploring the truth in family situations. Somebody is not being fair. You may still feel confused today and require some downtime to switch off. Look closely at your health today, as it's likely that you're feeling drained. Avoid self-medicating with dubious substances. Get some sleep instead.

Monday 18th

You feel the shift of both Jupiter and Mercury turning direct. Now is the time to pause, reflect and then attempt any salvaging of recent upsetting situations. Mars boosts your energy to do this, but don't run before you can walk. Rest first.

Tuesday 19th

A fiery Moon in your career sector helps you to navigate the day with confidence. The Moon opposes Mercury and could mean that your attention is required at work and in the home. You have the energy to get all the jobs done, but don't take on any extras. Enough is enough today.

Wednesday 20th

A Full Moon builds in your career sector. Your efforts will now be recognised and you may have completed projects to celebrate. This has felt like climbing an endless mountain but you are now at the top. Celebrate success and decide on a way forward from here.

Thursday 21st

From within your social sector, unrest bubbles. This isn't a bad thing, it's the rumblings of something new and exciting. Your groups are changing. You no longer need to hang out with those who don't bring you joy. You're more inclined to make friendships with those you can learn from.

Friday 22nd

Mars in your family sector is squaring off with Pluto retrograde in your relationships sector. You will need to find a way to balance the demands coming from these areas. It's tempting to switch off and have time alone, but this needs dealing with before the weekend begins.

Saturday 23rd

The Sun now moves into your sector of creativity, passion and romance. This can be a fun time if you let it. Your inner child wants to laugh and play. You have many niggling trains of thought over the weekend and this may bother you. Forget them, go and play.

Sunday 24th

You should find a way to relax today. The Moon in your hidden sector is causing agitation from a place deep inside of you. This can cause problems with your health if you aren't careful. Getting outside and working steadily through chores will help. Talk to a close friend or to your shadow.

Monday 25th

You're gifted with joy from Jupiter and energy from Mars, yet Neptune is coercing you into a fantasy land where you can be alone with your thoughts. Be active today, even if that's just chatting to people on social media. Get involved and perhaps you can laugh a little today.

Tuesday 26th

The Moon is now in your sign. A good connection from the Sun helps you express your needs and desires. This can be deep and intense. Someone special may witness this and a new level of understanding grows between you. Comfort foods will ease that ache to be nurtured.

Wednesday 27th

A battle between your heart and head is possible today. This will involve your close relationships where you may feel that there is no growth happening. Pause for a while and re-evaluate the worth of something if it is getting you down. Say no to what drains you.

Thursday 28th

Your pride is likely to kick in today. You're feeling irritable and protective of your self and what you've built around you. Venus and Jupiter make a nice connection in your duties and intimacy sectors. What you do for others does not go unrecognised today. You know who your true friends are.

Friday 29th

What is it that you value the most? Your home, bank balance and self-worth are all tied up with status today. A member from your social group may cause friction, but it's unlikely that you'll be slow to tell them. Discussing problems with family will help you now.

Saturday 30th

Mars enters your creative sector today. Your passion rises and you are driven to get things done to a high standard. Romantic liaisons will now be amped up by Mars in his own sign and looking for action. Do your research on a potential lover. Find out what makes them tick.

Sunday 31st

Conversations can be lusty today. Why not treat a lover to a tasty meal or a sensual experience. The intense Sun wants to rock your boat a little. Romance is strongly favoured if you play your cards right and be the best version of yourself now. Enjoy it.

NOVEMBER

. . . .

Monday 1st

There are moments today when you want to pack it all in and have some time alone. These are thankfully brief and you resist. Obligations to your close relationships are filled, keeping you in control of any changes you may have made. Happy chatter with family elders goes well.

Tuesday 2nd

Something has gone wrong in your personal relationships and this needs to be discussed, possibly with mediation or a third party. Today, you aim to get justice and fairness. Getting your point across can be tricky. Saturn will help if you remember to give thoughtful, considered responses and not to react hastily.

Wednesday 3rd

The Moon meets Mercury in your family sector. Many thoughts run through your head and you have an emotionally charged decision to make. Your heart is torn as this decision needs to be made with logic and rational thought. Make your case with compassion, but avoid sentimentality.

Thursday 4th

A New Moon in your creative sector asks you to start anew or seek refreshment in romantic relationships or creative projects. The energy surrounding this Moon is touchy. Mars gets involved and makes you irritable and maybe even angry. Uranus is also linked and this can mean disruption. Venus tries to help by skipping into your relationship sector.

Friday 5th

A deeply emotional Moon makes challenging connections today. There is no point holding on to something if it no longer serves you. If you cannot transform it for the better, let it go. Mercury enters your creative sector and will do some in-depth psychology on these issues.

Saturday 6th

The Moon hits the point of the karmic past. This confirms the need to move on from a challenging situation. Whilst Mercury tries to help Venus out and discover what the real issue is, Saturn asks that you be adult about it. Distract yourself with mundane duties for now.

Sunday 7th

Neptune is attempting to dissolve a belief you hold dear. You aren't ready for this and concern yourself with being busy and connecting to wider groups. You put energy into the wrong places and, by the end of the day, may feel guilty about this. Try not to burn out.

Monday 8th

The Moon enters your relationship sector and makes helpful connections to most planets. There is a way to resolve your troubles. The Moon and Venus make you more sensitive, compassionate and determined to make things work. Mars and Mercury at the beginning of your creative sector are helping you commit to this.

Tuesday 9th

You now look at things through the eyes of another. Where might you have projected your ideals onto someone else? Which part of your shadow is being illuminated now? It may be that your hidden parts are responsible for any unrest in your close relationships.

Wednesday 10th

Your rebellious streak may come out today. You find it hard to own your part in recent tension. Mercury and Mars meet and square off with Saturn and the Moon. The shell that you carry now protects your ego, but this may also have adverse effects. Hiding and sulking will only make matters worse.

Thursday 11th

Trying to justify yourself without apology leads to more unrest. Your social groups are now suffering and you may clash with someone who is bigger or more important than you. The current mood you are in is affecting all areas of your life. What can you do to resolve this?

Friday 12th

Today you take a long, hard look at where you have been responsible for upsetting people. Your shell softens and you begin to see another's point of view. Some fog should clear around these issues, making you able to see where you have been reluctant to apologise or conform.

Saturday 13th

A lovely, gentle Moon in your travel sector helps you to see the bigger picture. Spending the remainder of the weekend re-connecting with people is your priority. The Moon sits with Neptune and dissolves your anger, although Mercury has discovered something which may startle you. Is this the beginning of self-realisation?

Sunday 14th

Enjoy today, as there is better energy for you to relax and get back into balance with yourself. Connecting with others and discussing dreams, spirituality or travel will help you greatly. This will fire you up for the week to come. The positive side of change is becoming clear to you now.

Monday 15th

Just as you think you have things in control, outside influences come to unsettle you again. The Sun and Jupiter are clashing, as are the Moon and Venus. Your ego has likely been bashed again and you're begrudging trying to make amends. Sit tight and breathe deeply.

Tuesday 16th

Today you could solve this troublesome issue. Pluto, who resides in your relationship sector, is getting connections from both Sun and Moon today. You must try not to be led by your emotions or take things personally. The Sun will strengthen your resolve and give you strength and compassion for yourself.

Wednesday 17th

As the Moon shifts into your social sector, your attention turns towards friends. It's likely that you want to let off steam today or rant and rave. Your closest friends or even your online ones are willing to let you do this within a safe environment.

Thursday 18th

Is there a way that you can get creative with all this pent up angst inside you? Mars and Mercury in your creative sector are the perfect allies for getting things out of your system and out into the world. Writing, messy painting or a harsh session at the gym will help.

Friday 19th

A full moon in your social sector is the valve you have been waiting to open. This is the completion of a six-month phase or a realisation that something needs to go. Venus and Uranus are there to make a gentle, loving shift if need be.

Saturday 20th

Your mind will be extra busy now as the Moon is in your hidden sector. Intrusive thoughts still keep you awake at night, but this should be when you are more open to evaluating and processing them. Try not to dismiss any ideas you may have; note them all down and review objectively.

Sunday 21st

Another day of thoughtful inquiry is necessary today. You are slowly coming to terms with the recent upheavals. You desire to switch off and enjoy some downtime, but be careful not to do this by resorting to unhealthy coping mechanisms. These will only take you back to a place of muddy waters.

Monday 22nd

You begin the week settled, but still sensitive. The Moon is now in your sign and you find that your intuition is strong. Venus and Mars connect well, making it possible to enjoy a pleasant time with a loved one. The Sun moves into your health and duties sector.

Tuesday 23rd

Today, you have a need to take care of yourself and also meet the needs of a close relationship. Home comforts and good food may be the way forward. You are learning to put boundaries in place which will benefit the people on either side. Meeting in the middle does you good.

Wednesday 24th

You may have a moment when you are over-sensitive today. It is possible that you revert back to negative thinking. This afternoon, the Moon shifts and you smile again. Courage comes back to you and you should feel proud that you resisted the temptation to negate all your good self-work

Thursday 25th

Mercury has left your creative sector now. Did you notice all that mental activity when he was there? He now sits on the point of past karma and asks you to release the baggage before moving on. The winged messenger wishes you to fly unencumbered as he does. It's time to let things go.

Friday 26th

The Moon in your sector of value is making you see that your own self-worth is part of the problem. You undervalue yourself. Why do you think you are not good enough? A spiritual leader or person in authority is also trying to make you aware of this.

Saturday 27th

Despite all the self-analysis, you still doubt yourself. Have conversations with people close to you about this. In this case, siblings would be the best ones to talk to. You will realise how much you are loved, depended on and looked up to, simply because you are a sensitive soul.

Sunday 28th

Today you ponder the concepts of sacrifice and surrender. Do you do things for others because it is expected of you? Does this wear you down? Is this the reason for your poor self-image? If you're happy to serve others and you're rewarded, then it's no sacrifice.

Monday 29th

Family issues may require your attention and you're happy about this. The Moon makes great connections for networking and being your true self. Mercury has nothing to say today. You must listen and observe. Your energy is deep and intense. What will you learn today?

Tuesday 30th

Managing your family and personal relationships is not as easy, today. You may have to make promises to appease someone. Mercury and Saturn are talking about how you relate and behave in large groups. What is your role in the collective? Are you inspired to make a difference in the world?

DECEMBER

. . . .

Wednesday 1st

Exciting possibilities come back to you this afternoon. Neptune
turns direct and, finally, the fog clears. He has been sitting
in your travel sector, causing illusions and trying to drag you
away to fantasy land. Now those dreams of exploring new
cultures or exotic religions should move forward again.

Thursday 2nd

Intense discussions with a loved one provide food for thought.
A shared dream or wish can add fuel to your life together.
Thrashing through ideas for travel or an unusual work
vacation can be something which helps the two of you bond.
How far are you willing to go together?

Friday 3rd

The Moon meets Mars and you are unstoppable in your
passions. Perhaps you have found the very outlet that will
motivate you in love and in your personal development. This
afternoon, you're already making lists and ticking things off.
You're fired up from following a new direction.

Saturday 4th

A New Moon occurs in your health and duties sector. This is
fortunate, as it has coincided with your plans to do something
memorable. Mercury will help you do all the research now, as
he sits with the Moon and enjoys taking a leadership role.
Be careful to keep it real and manageable.

Sunday 5th

Your ideas and plans to get away, visit new lands or explore different cultures are getting huge now. Jupiter is linking to the Moon and expanding everything; your optimism, motivation and itinerary. Seeking the truth from around the wider world is what Jupiter wishes for you. Live it large.

Monday 6th

The Moon is now in your relationship sector and you are firmly resolute in your decision to do something exciting with a partner. You will take all the required steps to make this a real project. New plans are coming to you all the time. Start saving your pennies.

Tuesday 7th

Today you must take a good look at the finances required to bring your plan to manifestation. The Moon meets Pluto in your relationship sector and asks that you look at how joint finances can work to realise your shared dream. Explore every avenue possible now, before committing to one.

Wednesday 8th

A blockage or restriction is likely to stop you in your tracks today. This will be relatively minor, but enough to spoil your buoyant mood. Saturn wants to teach you something about acting too quickly. Find a person who has more knowledge and experience than you. Learn about possible pitfalls.

Thursday 9th

Don't run before you can walk. You're treading on new territory and you aren't the expert on it. Like a crab, side-step around this new ground and observe it before you head into it. Be armed with knowledge, and then you can gain wisdom.

Friday 10th

The Moon is now in your travel sector. Spend the weekend doing research by watching TV documentaries, reading books and looking at maps. You desire to merge with the collective and be a part of something special. Taking time to plan a short retreat may do you good and put you in the right mindset.

Saturday 11th

Venus and Pluto meet today in your relationship sector. This influence can be manipulative as both planets are connected to money. Venus needs you to remember what you've learned about your self-worth. Make sure that you and another person are on an equal footing in status and finances.

Sunday 12th

Your mind is so full of ideas that you can hardly contain them all. You need to decide which ones are 'pie in the sky' and which ones you can easily manage. The Sun is trying to help you expand your vision and not be blind-sided by illusions again.

Monday 13th

Mercury enters your relationship sector at the same time as Mars enters your health and duties sector. These shifts by inner planets will be more personal to you and you should take note. Let Mercury enhance your communication and Mars give you the energy for all the jobs you must do.

Tuesday 14th

Today you're more outwardly social and wish to connect with your wider groups. These can include online groups of people with the same interests as you. Conversations with friends can be lively and informative. Enjoy some luxury now; a tasty dinner or fine wine will suffice. You deserve it.

Wednesday 15th

The Moon meets Uranus today. The great disruptor can cause arguments to occur in your social circle, but can also cause the sort of friction which produces a pearl. You may find that your friendship groups come up with a valuable gem for you to take away and peruse.

Thursday 16th

Make the most of the Moon in your social sector. You will receive many benefits from these groups today. Neptune, Pluto and Venus connect, making this a dreamy time where you may be able to involve your lover. If single, love may come from these groups now.

Friday 17th

Mars is pumping the iron in your health and duties sector, he has his eye on the ball at all times. Unfortunately, your Mars-flavoured focus is opposed by the Moon in your hidden sector. Your mind will wander now. It will be hard to get back on track while the Moon is here.

Saturday 18th

The festive activities may have already begun and Venus, the planet of love, harmony, beauty and money goes retrograde. This will happen in your relationships house. Your love life may be wonky as you assess your value to each other. A lover from the distant past may return now.

Sunday 19th

Anxiety may get the better of you today. A full moon in your hidden sector can feel like all your deepest secrets are being exposed. Alternatively, you may now get some important insight into just one of the thoughts that have been keeping you awake at night.

Monday 20th

Today you may just need to have a duvet day eating ice cream and watching a favourite TV show. You cannot cope with other people's drama. Some of that drama may be coming from your own personal relationships as your head and heart do battle. See to your own needs today.

Tuesday 21st

The winter solstice today heralds the darkest night and the Sun's entry into your relationship sector. The promise of longer days to come will help to soothe any anguish you may be feeling with Venus in retrograde. Pluto reminds you that there are things you cannot control and you must let go.

Wednesday 22nd

This is a day for reflection. Saturn opposes the Moon and you may feel melancholy and low in spirits. There is energy available to you from Mars. Use this to get on with your mundane duties and take the opportunity to get ahead on your to-do list. There is plenty to prepare for the festive season.

Thursday 23rd

Jupiter has returned to the final degree of your intimacy sector. Consider with whom you have shared your deepest feelings this year. Has it been of value? Your pride is high today as you remember how you have allowed your shadow to surface and heal. You can carry that shell with honour.

Friday 24th

On this busy day, tempers rise and you may clash with people in charge. Everyone is overstretched and you just have to do your bit. Walk away from tension that has nothing to do with you. This is just the stress which accompanies this time of year, let it go and instead try to enjoy the season and all it brings.

Saturday 25th

Venus retrograde returns to meet Pluto today. A theme of manipulation and power struggles will play out. Once again, don't take this personally. You're the one who tries to maintain order by keeping communications going and reminding people of the reason for the celebrations.

Sunday 26th

Women's intuition and wisdom will win over any passive-aggression going on today. A gentle soul like yourself can be the one who keeps everything ticking along. Encourage talks with a loved one about the dreams you share. This will lighten the mood and give you something to look forward to.

Monday 27th

You have a balanced state of mind. Mars lends you the energy to go about the day. There are many places you need to be today; being organised will help you make each appointment you have. Your sense of responsibility is high and others notice this. Well done, you've turned around what could have been a disaster and course-corrected.

Tuesday 28th

It's likely that you've run out of steam and need to rest. The Moon in your family sector makes difficult connections to the planets in your relationship sector. You may see some effects of Venus retrograde now. This evening is romantic, but you're unlikely to be interested.

Wednesday 29th

Jupiter bounces into your travel sector. For the next twelve months, expect to find your guru, widen your world views and merge with the right kind of people who will help you grow and work towards your goals and dreams. Today, however, you may see disruption or surprises in your social sector. Cancel a date if you need to.

Thursday 30th

This can be a rather surreal day for you. Your head is full of chatter. This may be love talk, but there is an undertone which you aren't too happy about. It's dreamy and seductive but passive-aggression lies below the sweetness. Get a reality check now.

Friday 31st

On this last day of 2021, the Moon meets Mars in your health and duties sector. You are a powerhouse of energy and end the year with a bang. Stay sensible and congratulate yourself for getting through a tough year. Enjoy the celebrations tonight; you deserve it.

Cancer

....

DAILY FORECASTS
for 2022

JANUARY

. . . .

Saturday 1st

Happy New Year and welcome to 2022. The year begins
with some anticipation. You may be reviewing your duties
and priorities. Take it easy today, but try to combine your
important relationships with friendship and interest groups.
Practical or physical activity can be exhilarating and blow away
the cobwebs of last year.

Sunday 2nd

A new moon allows you to think about what you require
regarding love and partnerships. You might wish to learn more
about your relating patterns by taking things at a slower pace
and enjoying the journey. Deep enquiry and a need to share
may take a relationship to the next level.

Monday 3rd

Ghosts from the past may be playing with your heartstrings.
Perhaps there is still something outstanding which now needs
closure. It may be that you can't move on until this happens.
Don't be drawn into wishful thinking. Aim to be present with a
current relationship and give it all the attention it deserves.

Tuesday 4th

Emotions might prevent you from doing the right thing. Your
head and heart are in sync, but the focus could be wrong.
There are limits you might desire to breach, but you need to
think twice about this. Be responsible and respectful and you
may get back on track.

Wednesday 5th

Duty calls today. You could be quite busy and motivated to get your chores done. An outgoing approach helps you to connect with the job in hand. Make sure that you don't overdo things and wear yourself out as you may need time to unwind and do something nice for your wellbeing.

Thursday 6th

Dreams and fantasies can be huge today. This is good if you're enjoying free time and can indulge yourself. Travel plans might interest you as would higher education. Connecting with like-minded people could help to stir up ideas and inspire you to break free to do something unusual.

Friday 7th

Today can be extra dreamy and your energy to do practical work could leak out. A yearning to be back in time when things seemed easier may fill you. This is an illusion and can consume you if you're not careful. Draw a line under the past and move on.

Saturday 8th

Your focus may shift, and you become more productive as the day progresses. Plans for the new year may be discussed with a partner. Doing something for the greater good or taking a leadership role may suit you now. Where can you be your own boss? Make enquiries.

Sunday 9th

This may be a pivotal day where you need to face a troubling issue with love or money. There could be a crucial piece of information you're missing. Don't be tempted to act without it. You may be moody or depressed today and come across as very needy. Do something invigorating instead.

Monday 10th

You could be reluctant to change a plan or your way of doing things. However, progress may not be possible until you do. Seek help from your friendship groups as they may be able to ground you and give you practical advice. Think outside the box to get results.

Tuesday 11th

Today can feel confusing. You might have an idea of where your inner compass is taking you, but as yet, it doesn't appeal. It can be hard to fix on any one thing as nothing is giving you the sense of security you need right now. Wait until you have clarity.

Wednesday 12th

Your emotions are visible to all today. Ensure that you have dealt with love and money issues. They may be impacting on your self-worth. If you feel a little lost or out of sorts, try doing practical work or bringing your attention back to your current relationship.

Thursday 13th

Retreating into your private thoughts can give you the time you need to process awkward emotions. Search your soul for reasons why these emotions have been triggered. Mercury turns retrograde tomorrow, so make all the necessary preparations. Back up devices, double check travel plans and aim for clear communication.

Friday 14th

You might decide to do your personal investigations today. However, Mercury may soon prevent any further clarity and you can become more muddled and frustrated. Go with the flow and be adaptable. Take in as much information as you need, but file it away to be processed later on.

Saturday 15th

The Moon arrives in your sign and can make you overly sensitive or intuitive now. You might feel drained of energy and prefer a relaxed weekend alone. If you seek company, ensure they can provide you with a nurturing environment and food for your soul. You may witness a permanent ending.

Sunday 16th

Be good to yourself now. You may find numerous triggers going off within you and could feel defensive. Stay in your shell if you need to, but remember that you still have to deal with this. It may be that your habits and conditioned behaviour are letting you down.

Monday 17th

A full moon in your sign may highlight what makes you feel safe and what feels like an attack. Tricky planetary energy can make you feel vulnerable and unloved. This may make you reach to a past which has long gone or an old dream which no longer serves you.

Tuesday 18th

Uranus turns direct today and can help you switch things up and be more innovative in your interest groups. You could be more willing to speak your mind, play and have fun. Remember that you need to be extremely clear when communicating. This may be a problem during the evening.

Wednesday 19th

What can you do to bring more warmth to a love relationship? You could find yourself stuck between a rock and a hard place today. You might wish to be unconventional or simply do something different but hit obstacles. Bring the cosiness closer to home and be traditional instead.

Thursday 20th

You might get more luck if you wish to express yourself clearly today. This could come from paying attention to detail and filtering your speech before speaking aloud. Don't let yourself be taken for granted as your good nature may be perceived as a weakness now and that won't help your self-esteem.

Friday 21st

Get ready to think outside the box and solve the problems associated with money or self-love today. Practical application, exercise or a course of study can help you work your way through this. Try to keep emotions out of it and you may find that the results are what you need.

Saturday 22nd

An illusion you've been harbouring could dissolve today and you see someone or something in their true colours. Conversations may be tricky due to Mercury retrograde, but if you remember this and take extra time, you may see that the change or ending you've been avoiding is the very thing needed now.

Sunday 23rd

You would be wise to be an observer today and let everything around you play itself out. Listen carefully to your intuition as it may be sending you subtle messages. Allow yourself to feel the emotions without activating a response. You could be in a stalemate situation and need time to think.

Monday 24th

Mars enters your relationship zone. This can herald a time where your relating patterns come under fire. It could also add zest and make your sex drive higher. As Mars will meet Venus here, this is one possible effect. It could also lead to battles and power struggles.

Tuesday 25th

Be prepared for an intense day of mixed emotions. There might be trouble within friendship groups which stunts your creativity. You could also have many romantic or artistic ideas now but can't seem to get them implemented. Satisfaction or gratification will not come by trying too hard.

Wednesday 26th

This is a precarious time as there are now two retrograde planets in your relationship zone. You will need to be extra aware of how you're communicating and asking for loving. If you come across as too much, then it will blow up in your face. Be respectful and be true to your own values.

Thursday 27th

Harking back to past times might just make you all the more reluctant to deal with current problems. Try to get through the day by being of service to others and showing that you're willing to learn and go the extra mile. Reach out beyond your comfort zone.

Friday 28th

You might be more outgoing and curious today. Something may attract you and you wish to know more about it. This could be an inspirational act of goodness, a teacher or a culture which you would like to know more about. The world is out there waiting to be discovered.

Saturday 29th

Venus turns direct now. You might experience this as a lightening of your load. A ghost from the past may disappear back to where it belongs and may no longer bother you. Be alert and you may find a new mission which can inspire you to be driven and productive.

Sunday 30th

It's possible that you reaffirm your relationship and vow to make it your priority. Be sure that your partner is on board with this as you could become suffocating and frighten them off. Switching things up at this stage can be premature, so look for guidance and act accordingly.

Monday 31st

Take time today to stop, look and listen to what is really going on for you. Remember that Mercury is still retrograde, and you could be digging a hole for yourself which will be left like an open wound. Don't leave yourself vulnerable to attack or rejection. Think twice before committing to anything.

FEBRUARY

· · · · · · · · · · · · · · · · · ·

Tuesday 1st

A new moon allows you to set goals regarding intimacy, shared finances and interest groups. You might find that you wish to do some work which could be unusual. It may mean exploring the depths of how you can be of service to the world. Good causes can attract you.

Wednesday 2nd

The urge to travel or connect with people from other cultures may see you making vacation plans with a partner. Should you wish to do this, start making solid plans and do all your research. You might find a romantic getaway appeals to both of you.

Thursday 3rd

Your natural sensitivity stretches far today. Empathy and love can inspire you to open your heart a little more and take down some defences. You may have a new way of relating which you would like to explore with someone who shares your need for harmony and pleasure.

Friday 4th

Mercury turns direct today and continues his path through your relationship zone. This is useful if there are things you both need to discover and learn. This is a dreamy time and you could have many ideas you wish to put to a partner. Let them have their say too.

Saturday 5th

There may be no time for dreaming or romancing as you have work to do. It's likely that you have hit a snag and need to come back to reality. Look at what your limits are, both in finances and obligations. Be reasonable and follow your mind rather than your emotions now.

Sunday 6th

If there is too much going on in your head, focus on what is essential and leave the rest for another time. You could be putting too much on yourself or thinking up idealistic notions which aren't attainable. You might need to scrap your plans or make some minor adjustments.

Monday 7th

Your friendship groups may be helpful if you are seeking advice. This might be about relating but may also give you fresh ideas about building something solid. However, there is unstable energy which can make you irritable or anxious to get started on a project. Use it wisely.

Tuesday 8th

This is a challenging day where you may need to avoid being too emotionally attached to things. If something doesn't feel right or is continuously evading you, it's not meant for you. Leave it alone and look instead to where your inner compass is guiding you. Align with your core values.

Wednesday 9th

Some time for introspection would be good for you. The future beckons and asks that you change your stance from emotions to more practical things. If you want something badly enough, you must take the necessary steps and get it for yourself. Take time to get things straight in your mind.

Thursday 10th

You may have conflicting thoughts today. Some will concern expanding your work prospects whilst others make you doubt yourself. You should follow the path of the doubts and discover why you feel that way. You may learn something to your advantage. A boss or teacher could give you good advice.

Friday 11th

Your romantic relationships may have a lesson for you. Listen carefully and you may hear an invitation to go on a new mission. You might have experienced many changes in recent years, and this may be another one. What do you need to let go of in order to grow?

Saturday 12th

The celestial lovers, Mars and Venus are getting close in your relationship zone. This is a sure sign that a new cycle is starting. Try not to take any emotional baggage on this new journey as it will weigh you down. You may be excited about the prospects this can promise.

Sunday 13th

Today you might fall back on old habits and conditioning. Self-doubt creeps in and your self-esteem may hit a low point. Shake yourself out of this. This might be the excess baggage you must leave behind. You should nurture yourself and feed your own soul now. Protect your soft inner core.

Monday 14th

This morning you could have a sense of grief after a loss. Honour what that meant to you and let it go with love. You are about to search your soul for answers and your wider interest groups can encourage and support this. Speak from the heart and be courageous.

Tuesday 15th

If you don't want to challenge the status quo, stay indoors and hide. If you would prefer to evolve and become a better version of you, come out and face it. It is this kind of irritation which makes the pearl. You can't shine your light if you are hiding.

Wednesday 16th

Mark this day as auspicious. Mars and Venus meet under a full moon. You could feel playful and wish to enjoy some pleasure. Come out of your shell and embrace the passion that is being offered. A partnership may reach a new level where you understand the meaning of unconditional love.

Thursday 17th

Get touchy and feely today as the energy is tactile and you should engage with it. Yoga, physical exercise or the great outdoors can lift you up. Something might rock your world today and this may be sexual or spiritual. Stay grounded and in touch with your environment.

Friday 18th

Your inner compass seems to have shifted. Get back into alignment and see where your true north is now. It could be that your focus has changed, and different things are important. You may understand better the need to let go of dead weight and be in the present.

Saturday 19th

Family matters might be on the agenda this weekend. These may involve a serious talk with members or a conference in which you come to an agreement. This is nothing to worry about and it could be that a long-standing issue has been resolved. Let everyone have their say.

Sunday 20th

Don't be put off by perceived blockages. It could be that family life and partner time clash. This will pass, and you're advised to prioritise and explain to each side that you have obligations. Don't beat yourself up trying to come to a balance as you will be the one who suffers.

Monday 21st

Today might be intense and emotional. This can be positive, so don't take anything personally. It simply means that your intuition is working well and you're picking up on the atmosphere around you. If you're creative, you may find a muse today and put pen to paper for a loved one.

Tuesday 22nd

Love and passion are on the agenda today, so make sure that you keep in contact with your romantic partner. You could feel frustrated and impatient to see them this evening. Watch out for a misty glow from your inner compass, which can entice you into sensual and surreal experiences.

Wednesday 23rd

Some changes are necessary today and you might dislike having to implement them at first. However, when you can see how beneficial this will be, you are driven and can act responsibly. These changes can open up new opportunities you haven't noticed before. Follow where they lead and don't miss out.

Thursday 24th

Look to the horizon and imagine yourself there. Expand your mind and see yourself further from home. You might need to come out of your comfort zone now or these new opportunities will pass you by. Stay sensible but embrace what the future is offering you. This is your moment.

Friday 25th

You could be having second thoughts and doubting yourself again. Try to understand that these were coping mechanisms which kept you safe when you were young, but you've outgrown them, and they need to go. You're the one holding yourself back. Discuss this with a supportive partner.

Saturday 26th

Learn to recognise that the irritation in your shell is what is asking you to grow. There are plenty of blessings for you now, so be brave and accept them. Interest groups can provide you with unusual solutions or new ways of being able to connect and still feel safe.

Sunday 27th

This is a lovely day where your ruler, the Moon, meets both Mars and Venus who are still together in your relationship zone. You may feel passionate and emotionally attached to a partner and a shared dream. Maybe your partner can also feel this. This is a new cycle, so enjoy it.

Monday 28th

Everything is in place for you to love and grow this year. If you're restless, find a positive outlet for that energy. Conversations with a partner can lead to a deeper discovery of each other and you may be stunned at how in sync you are.

MARCH
·················

Tuesday 1st

Today you must find a workaround for a problem. Higher education or something from other cultures might provide the answers. Friendship groups can also be a source of inspiration and allow you to explore many possibilities. Give gratitude where it's due and you will be helped again another time.

Wednesday 2nd

A new moon offers you a chance to make the right connections today. Note who enters your life now as they may be significant in six months. Relationships might be going through positive changes and a restructuring of your shared life is possible. You could be talking to legal advisers.

Thursday 3rd

Your ruler, the Moon, meets Neptune, your inner compass. You are in perfect alignment. It may be that your love life is rather dreamy right now and you're excited about reaching a new level of understanding which complies with your vision of the future. Honour the path that has led you here.

Friday 4th

Use today to come down from cloud nine and think about career goals. There may be much to do here, but you have the necessary energy to focus and get things done. Your enthusiasm can lift others and teamwork becomes a pleasurable activity for all involved.

. . . .

Saturday 5th

Make sure that there is nothing you need to do regarding your relationship. It's possible that something has been overlooked and you may need to finalise this today. There are many blessings to be had, so watch out for what is being offered and grab it. Travel and education are favoured.

Sunday 6th

If doubt creeps in and spoils your current mood, dismiss it and keep looking to the future. Mars and Venus have entered your intimacy sector together and shared finances and the deeper mysteries of life become important. A celebration may be organised with friends and interest groups. Host a party.

Monday 7th

You could be bursting with emotions or ideas for a new life. This might be a new home or job. Money and life's little pleasures seem more attainable now than they have for a long time. You could come up against a roadblock this evening, but you will find a way through it.

Tuesday 8th

Keep your feet on the ground today as you might be tempted to run before you can walk. Pay attention to details regarding contracts or other such commitments. You could have a lot to process this evening which could keep you awake tonight. Share this with your partner.

Wednesday 9th

There is high activity in your intimacy zone now and there could be outstanding or fiddly things to deal with. You might need to call upon a professional for help. Logic and reason are needed now but you may be too emotionally attached to do this yourself. Stay calm and optimistic.

Thursday 10th

You could be noticing that new contacts are coming from all around the world. A soul family may be forming of people with similar interests. Today you must see to the daily grind and put your dreamy, sensitive soul to one side. There is work to be done.

Friday 11th

The Moon in your sign makes you more sensitive and intuitive. If you need to talk business or simply connect with new people, you will be more inclined towards empathy and understanding. Be mindful of how you come across. Caring is fine, but over-caring becomes smothering and won't be appreciated.

Saturday 12th

You could have an air of optimism today and get a lot done, although you may be feeling the need to nest or have some time at home. Perhaps you're making home improvements or strengthening your security. Whatever it is, you could be feeling more at home this weekend.

Sunday 13th

Take a good look at your inner compass today. Any mists have now shifted, and you could have perfect clarity. Is it still what you want? Stay in control and don't be swayed into doing something which doesn't feel right. An evening in your own home can make you feel like royalty.

Monday 14th

You might desire to retreat into your shell today. You could be feeling defensive or threatened by a small upset. This isn't as serious as you think and will pass soon. Don't risk an argument by being self-righteous or greedy. Something could erupt or be unstable this evening.

Tuesday 15th

Today brings some challenges that you need to work through or leave well alone until your mood is better. You could be pushing against the flow and this tactic won't get you anywhere. Try looking at the problems objectively. Find a creative or an innovative solution and ask for help.

Wednesday 16th

You would be wise to check every tiny detail today. Communications will benefit from absolute clarity and you will know where you stand on certain issues. It may be possible to call upon siblings or close friends and do something that requires both sides giving unconditional service to each other.

Thursday 17th

Your sensitive nature may feel that it's being taken for granted today. This is habitual behaviour and needs addressing. However, this is a passing Moon phase, which can make you feel disconnected from yourself and is not the fault of others. Stand as an observer to your own responses.

Friday 18th

This morning's full moon can illuminate any troubles you have regarding your health or being of service to others. If you recognise an issue, today may be the right time to change it or transform it into something more beneficial. Aim for balance and equality within your family this weekend.

Saturday 19th

Emotional satisfaction can help to bring family and intimate partners together in the same room. A group get-together might cause some anticipation but may not be as bad as you think. Be respectful and responsible to all and your sensitive nature can guarantee a happy time with those you love.

Sunday 20th

The spring equinox arrives, and you can look forward to longer days. This period may also enhance your work prospects and give you food for thought. Think of your mind waking up and exploding with ideas you wish to implement. Get creative and sensual and enjoy an evening of romance.

Monday 21st

You might need to watch what you say today as conversations could get out of hand and escalate quickly. It's possible that you feel attacked from every angle, so retreat under your shell if you need to. It's more than okay to protect yourself under these circumstances.

Tuesday 22nd

Romantic and creative pursuits could come under fire now.
Things may not be ticking along the way you wish. Time
for yourself can help you to process deep feelings and avoid
unnecessary conflict. If you choose to engage, you may be
inviting an explosion of volcanic proportions into your world.

Wednesday 23rd

It's important to listen to your inner voice today. Your true north
is asking you to get back into alignment. A partner may be of great
value now as a voice of reason and logic. You could be too emotional
to work this out by yourself. Watch for any and every opportunity.

Thursday 24th

You might have another day filled with challenges. If reaching
out and broadening your horizons is feeling like an arduous
task, just do your necessary chores without over-stretching
yourself. You have limitations too and doing more than you
should will make you drained or unwell. Go easy on yourself.

Friday 25th

Egos and emotions may clash today, so step back and get some
breathing space. Partnerships may be strained. Patience is
needed now, or you may find yourself back at a starting point
after already completing a hard climb. Your efforts will be
rewarded if you take things slower this time.

Saturday 26th

Communications can be better today as you aim to fix or
improve on something which isn't working. You might see the
need for change or adjustment and do your best to implement
this. By evening you may be more satisfied with how things
look now. Your head and heart are in sync.

Sunday 27th

Your energy turns introspective but also attaches to the outside world. You might have great compassion for a good cause or something which is unfair and unjust. This can play on your mind and you wish to explore it more. Perhaps there is something you can do to help.

Monday 28th

Today you might be filled with the need to be a compassionate warrior. Under this energy, you may wish to start a revolution or lead the way in making a big change in your community. You could also bring it closer to home and upgrade your relationships with a firm commitment.

Tuesday 29th

Be mindful of sensitive dreamy energy which can make your recent thinking less tangible. You might need to keep one foot on the ground before you wander off into wishful thinking or ideas which could become overwhelming. Try not to drown in the sea of possibilities you may be in.

Wednesday 30th

Floaty energy continues but is aided now by finding your inner compass. This can anchor your thoughts and help you see if what has stirred you is in alignment with your true values. You can have more optimism and others will be attracted to that. You may start a revolution.

Thursday 31st

Today you might be more fired up than usual and wish to make changes. This may mean letting something go which hasn't brought you any benefits. Level the playing field and make space for new growth. You could be unstoppable now and others will be trying to catch up.

APRIL
. . . .

Friday 1st

A new moon is an excellent opportunity to ask for what you want at work. It may be you who has the best plans for a new project. If this is something you are passionate about, speak to those in charge and get it off the ground.

Saturday 2nd

Although you have your heart set on a new project, you might find it difficult to make some of the necessary changes. However, stick to your guns and plant your ideas in solid ground. Accept the advice and wisdom of your elders or others who have more experience.

Sunday 3rd

It's especially important that you listen to your intuition today. You could have a revelation and find a solution to a problem. Try not to communicate this just yet, but give yourself time to process it thoroughly in your own mind. Innovation is the key to doing this thing well.

Monday 4th

You might wish to lie low today and do some groundwork. There could be many challenges that you have to work through, but this will look good on your resume. Keep emotionally detached and you might get the results you require. Try not to push if it isn't going at your pace.

Tuesday 5th

You might be able to accept an ending or a change today. This could play out in your relationships and will likely be a positive one. The energy suggests that you can put a lot of energy into what you're passionate about and get the respect you deserve.

Wednesday 6th

Communications and networking might be on fire today. You could find the contacts you need who can enhance a new project. Your mental juices may be overflowing with ideas. Once again, try not to get out of your depth and ask for help if you need it. Keep it real.

Thursday 7th

Your emotions might be tested today. However, this only means that you have no time for daydreaming or unattainable projects. Stick to the job in hand and get all your research done as you will need this in the near future. This evening you can relax with a loved one.

Friday 8th

Settle in for a cosy weekend with a partner or some quality time for yourself. The energy is intimate and nurturing. You can dream to your heart's content with great company and favourite foods. This can be food for your soul too, so lap it up and share your comfort zone.

Saturday 9th

Stay under your duvet and make the most of this floaty, romantic energy. If you have a muse, create some art. There are many blessings to be accessed today which could include travel opportunities or getting to know people from distant lands. Open your heart and expand your mind.

Sunday 10th

Today you must speak your truth if you find yourself in a confrontation. Think of what holds value for you and accept nothing less than quality. You might need to have a difficult discussion with a partner. Be kind and compassionate, but stay strong and try not to compromise your values.

Monday 11th

You might find it easier to ground your plans now. Search through your friendships and interest groups for connections who can help. You could experience an unwelcome trigger which challenges your personal truth. However, there is good news about travel, education and merging with the collective which may lift your spirits.

Tuesday 12th

Keep an eye on your energy levels today. You might find it seeping away on futile projects. This could have an effect on your health, so take time this evening to be good to yourself and give yourself quality time. Mundane chatting with friends can help you relax and chill out.

Wednesday 13th

There may be a feeling that the things you desire are evading you. Maybe you aren't desiring the right things. If something is meant for you it will be available. You may need to sit with a pen and paper and make lists or get methodical about some of your plans.

Thursday 14th

Don't waste your breath asking for the Moon. Although she is your ruler, you may be extending your limits and boundaries too far. Alternatively, you could be spending energy by doing things for others. Stay aware and notice who is taking you for granted as this has to stop now.

Friday 15th

There are now four planets in your travel and education zone. You may have more inspiration and a bigger urge to merge with people who can inspire you to stretch your mind and learn more. However, you could also be tempted to take too much on and risk burnout.

Saturday 16th

A full moon throws the spotlight on your family and roots. Look at the balance now and decipher where there could be more or less contribution. You might have completed a family project and there is cause for celebration. Hosting and nurturing loved ones can remind you how much you're blessed.

Sunday 17th

Intense energy can bring out your creative side. If you feel romantic or artistic then act now and get deeply involved with pursuing what you regard as beauty. You might border on the erotic or exotic and look for real and meaningful muses to bring out this part of you.

Monday 18th

It's possible that your dreams have been vivid, or you have had a sleepless night. You could have many thoughts to process, but they might be too intense to share. Something from the past might enter your awareness and you may need to let it go once and for all.

Tuesday 19th

If you come out of your shell today, beware of being over-assertive. You may feel outgoing but come across as pushy and belligerent. Others will not be too pleased with your insistence on marching into their lives. March on your own territory for a while and scan the horizon.

Wednesday 20th

It's important that you listen to your elders today. Put your dreams to one side and get all your mundane duties done. If you find that this is distracting you from your deeper vision, ask yourself why. It may simply be that there is work to be done elsewhere.

Thursday 21st

Your significant relationships come into focus now. You might wish to make the most of grounding energy to do something practical together. Planning a future trip can give you both an air of excitement and something to look forward to. Be flexible and aim for something you wouldn't usually do.

Friday 22nd

This is a lovely day for connecting with people from outside your community. There could be something which has got your interest that you'd like to pursue. Online interest groups may also be a source of knowledge and can support you in your endeavours. Be bold and brave. Try something new.

Saturday 23rd

You may feel more devoted now and wish to join in a venture which takes you to levels you have yet to experience. This might feel uncomfortable at first, but you will soon see the benefits of stepping outside your comfort zone. Research may be needed and can be intriguing.

Sunday 24th

It's possible that you feel out of your depth, but you won't know until you give it a go. You could feel thwarted or experience some resistance. This is probably coming from within you and is a natural response. Watch what you say to people in charge of proceedings.

Monday 25th

Try to assess what your own limits are if you feel inadequate. You might be trying to connect with something which isn't right for you. This afternoon you may have more idea if this is true. An emotional attachment is important to you and if that's not there you should back away.

Tuesday 26th

You could wake up as if you had run a marathon in your sleep. Give yourself extra time to process things today and don't take on anything new. When you've had space to think, you may have an 'aha!' moment and all will become clear. Reward yourself for this.

Wednesday 27th

Your dreams return to you in glorious technicolour. Reconnecting with your inner compass may come as a relief now. Expect to be swept off your feet with renewed motivation and a willingness to stay aligned with your true values. There are blessings to be had in education and travel.

Thursday 28th

Look back to the start of the year when you might have had a revelation about your new mission or future path. You may see the signpost ahead of you beckoning you on. Solid foundations are needed for you to feel secure and able to march onwards to your destiny.

Friday 29th

Pluto turns retrograde today. This can herald a period of new beginnings and also endings. If there's something you have been reluctant to let go of, but know you should, it will be released at this time. Something in your social circle may need urgent attention.

Saturday 30th

A new moon and solar eclipse open a window of wild card energy within your friendship groups. Expect the unexpected but refrain from leading a revolution. Mercury enters the deepest part of your psyche now and will root around for those pearls you've been hiding. You may experience some old wounds being reopened.

MAY

....

Sunday 1st

You could experience a sense of urgency today. There might be
a shift in your relationships or something which needs dealing
with quickly before it escalates. This energy may also mean
that long distance connections need attention or that a travel
plan needs to be finalised or paid for.

Monday 2nd

A head full of chatter can make for a restless day. You could be
trying to process something deep in your psyche. If clarity is
nowhere to be found, listen to your heart. It might be difficult
to discern your inner critic from your inner cheerleader, so
talking about it may help.

Tuesday 3rd

Today your energy and thoughts could be all over the place.
You might be too scattered to focus on any one thing. Learn to
be flexible today and go with the flow. You may end up down a
rabbit hole, but you could also discover something whilst you
are there.

Wednesday 4th

A lot of unstable energy might threaten to derail you, but this
could also be the impetus you need to get something done.
You may not feel much like connecting to others today and
would do better by getting your head down and dealing with
the daily grind.

Thursday 5th

Look out for a light bulb or a beacon today. Your social groups could come up with an ingenious idea or plan which may bring a new meaning or a new journey. This could be ground-breaking so follow it up. There may be trouble with females in the workplace.

Friday 6th

You might have more self-love today and might nurture your inner child. Forgiveness for your past deeds may be necessary and welcomed. A lovely mixture of compassion, enquiry and dedicated action may help you to solve a riddle or change behaviour patterns that no longer work for you.

Saturday 7th

This is a great day for speaking your truth. This can also be a sort of therapy which lead you on a healing path. Your emotions may be big, and you wear them on your sleeve today. If you get an insight or revelation from your psyche, treat it as a pearl of wisdom.

Sunday 8th

Fiery energy spurs you on today. You might see some changes in your workplace attitude. This may also involve a financial gain or a more comfortable working environment. Try not to show off or claim leadership within your social groups today as it could easily end in tears or splits.

Monday 9th

You could be quite stubborn today and as a defence mechanism you may be a little rebellious and rub up against authority. Mercury turns retrograde tomorrow, so use your restless energy to prepare. Back up all devices, double-check travel plans and don't sign anything for now.

Tuesday 10th

Communications may instantly feel the effect of Mercury retrograde. You must be methodical and discerning in all conversations both written and spoken. Details could be missing, and this can make you frustrated. Mercury will go back over your private zone and resurrect things which need to surface and be healed. This may be uncomfortable.

Wednesday 11th

Stay alert for new opportunities in the workplace. They may not be ready yet, but you could see something which is worth putting in the diary for later. Long-distance communication or study can drain you today and you won't do your best work. Leave it until this feeling passes.

Thursday 12th

Today you might feel the need to check in with your family or go back to the start of an old tradition. You could have some ideas which you wish to resurrect. Pitch the ideas first and let others dwell on them for a while.

Friday 13th

Dividing your attention between work and home may cause some conflict. Prioritise and do what's essential before allowing yourself some downtime with your tribe. Friendship or interest groups may provide food for thought and give you an outlet for something you have been interested in pursuing. Perhaps this is a practical or money-making idea.

Saturday 14th

Your important relationships are shifting or having a clear-out.
You might not like how this upsets the status quo, but it's a
necessary process to clear the decks for new growth. Getting
romantic and sensual together can help distract from any
mundane or legal issues you have going on.

Sunday 15th

Intense energy may be building between your romance and
friendship groups. You might need to consider blending them
somehow. Sharing your dreams with your wider groups can be
the way to get any groundwork or research done. This might
antagonise a partner as they may feel left out.

Monday 16th

An intense full moon and a lunar eclipse can signify an end to
a recent issue concerning romance and creativity. You could
come under fire now and may need to rethink a strategy. This
can be a tricky day if you're back-pedalling on an agreement.
Ensure clear communication without hurting anyone.

Tuesday 17th

Today is slightly easier as you have the right attitude towards
work. It could be that money or harmony has come in and lit
a new fire for you to be cosy by. New responsibilities can mean
that you use more empathy and compassion in your working
role. This may please you greatly.

Wednesday 18th

You might have an itch that needs scratching and you just can't reach it. This frustrates you and can mean that you need to change your perspective for any progress to occur. A partner may help you to offload your concerns and make an action plan with bite-size steps.

Thursday 19th

You can be quite productive today if you keep your mind on task. Partner time may also benefit as you feel as if you are working together to reap rewards you can share. Check your bank balance today and refrain from making an impulse buy you will regret later.

Friday 20th

Any disturbances in your psyche can feel huge today. You could feel extra sensitive and defensive. Tears may be close to the surface as something you should have let go a long time ago leaves of its own accord. You must think of the broader picture now and not dwell on your loss.

Saturday 21st

Today you are being asked to go within and light up your darkest corners. You might feel some resistance to this as you dislike being exposed. You may feel vulnerable or not willing to get deep and wide in things you don't understand. Listen out for a helpful guide.

Sunday 22nd

You could have a day where necessary chores take precedence. You must be responsible and get them done. This evening your mood might become more emotional and you need time alone to process your feelings. Don't force a conversation or any inner work. Let it come naturally to be healed.

Monday 23rd

Long distance contacts and friendship groups can be
supportive now. You could be returning to an event or issue
from the recent past which needs evaluation. Don't be in a
rush to find a solution or your energy may seep out in the
wrong direction. Be gentle with yourself.

Tuesday 24th

Your inner compass is within sight and you might wish to
anchor yourself to it. A conflict between wanting to drift or
wanting motivation to engage upsets you. Travel, research
or higher education may give clues or satisfy your need to be
productive. Stay in your safety zone and work from a distance.

Wednesday 25th

A small shift regarding your work may occur. You might find
the motivation or new stimulus you've been searching for. This
can come as a new teacher or guide. You may be asked to use
your mental and emotional faculties to work on something for
the greater good.

Thursday 26th

An energetic shift can have you working relentlessly today.
You could be aiming to impress someone important who
could make great changes for you. However, you must play
by the rules and be completely respectful. There may be some
important lessons for you. Missing these may mean missing
out on an opportunity.

Friday 27th

The early hours may keep you awake with thoughts of your newfound responsibilities. You might need to factor in how this will affect a relationship. Be proactive and make the changes or endings that are needed now. Spend the day being productive and planting seeds for future endeavours.

Saturday 28th

There's a lot of shaking up occurring in your social arena now. Venus has joined in and will bring in some financial gain or more reason to enjoy your participation here. It could be that you will be standing up for the underdog and offering a compassionate ear to all.

Sunday 29th

Your career is also set for new activity and you could be taking on a huge new role. There are some challenges today, but you must learn not to rise to them. Instead, be a passive observer and watch how they play out without you. You might be satisfied with the change.

Monday 30th

A new moon in your private sector can give you food for thought. Set goals and intentions regarding your own inner growth. Leave yourself room for improvement and be flexible and realistic. This could also herald a time where you learn to laugh and play more than you've done recently.

Tuesday 31st

Get your head down and concentrate on your most important tasks. You may be watched by an elder or person in charge and will need to make a good impression. Your dreams and ambitions might need an overhaul in the coming months as so much has changed in your daily life.

JUNE
....

Wednesday 1st

You might feel more like yourself today, but this also means that you could be overly sensitive to criticism. Although this may not be meant negatively, you could take it that way. Focus on something which is filling you with joy and enthusiasm. Your social groups perhaps.

Thursday 2nd

The right frame of mind will yield the right results. You could be using your new role within groups and making waves. Bring your natural nurturing self to the group and you might see that this produces a sense of teamwork and belonging for all involved.

Friday 3rd

Mercury is direct now and is finishing his work in your social arena. You might have found new meaning and can now commit to a new project. This may also mean that changes are due in your one to one relationship and these can come at a price. Stay true to your personal path.

Saturday 4th

Saturn turns retrograde now. The greatest teacher of the planets will have some lessons for you. You could be searching far and wide for answers or methods which you can apply to your work and groups. Boundaries will become a theme and you might need to strengthen your own.

Sunday 5th

Be careful who you deal with today and the tone in which you express yourself. What holds quality and value for you may not be the same for others. There could be some glory to be had by speaking your truth, but only if it is sincere, kind and honest.

Monday 6th

You might be looking for information which can help you decipher a few things you have lately become interested in. If you're curious, learn how to discern fact from fiction and get straight to the facts. Interactions might be unconditional but may also be burdensome. Remember your boundaries.

Tuesday 7th

Group ventures could fill your mind today. Be careful as this might be a tactic you're using to distract from something private that is niggling you. Leave time in the day to process what is bothering you. This could also be a health problem which you have been ignoring.

Wednesday 8th

Grounding activities would suit you best now. Practical application of tasks or writing a 'to do' list can help you with changes you find difficult. You may need to emotionally detach yourself before any progress can be made. Try to be fair and if you feel grieved, look to your family for support.

Thursday 9th

Problems may seem bigger than they are today. However, this doesn't stop you from being drained and possibly ill. If you need a break, ask for it. You could be overworked and not spending enough time with your home and family. Come back to your centre to work this out.

Friday 10th

Mental stimulation may give you a headache if you aren't careful. It may also show you that one of your life lessons is beginning. You must put yourself first for a change. See to your own needs before offering your services. Set your personal boundaries and protect your energy.

Saturday 11th

Stick to practical jobs today as they distract you from unwanted thoughts and emotions. Self-care and support from like-minded people can be the remedies you need. If you must, give others a shock by being more assertive and selfish today. Let them know you mean business and today is for you.

Sunday 12th

You could have intense feelings about detaching from energy suckers today. It may go against your nature to do your own thing, but sometimes it's necessary. Your mood can fluctuate, but you need to stay true to yourself now. Finalise something concerning learning within your friendship groups.

Monday 13th

You could be more outgoing and passionate about your work today. Mundane chores and your professional work can be done to a high standard. Mercury returns to your private thoughts to help you continue the search for gold. You might have good qualities that you've been afraid to show the world.

Tuesday 14th

The full moon today can illuminate what you've done in the areas of routine and general health. It can also show where you're stretching your boundaries and desiring to learn more about other cultures. There might be a completion or a discarding of a mundane chore.

Wednesday 15th

You could get into battle with someone big and brash today. This might be an ego clash and you could resort to hiding in your shell or attacking with pincers out. It can also be that your sensitivity towards a partnership clashes with what is going on workwise. You may need to prioritise.

Thursday 16th

It's possible that you wake feeling irritable and need to expel some restless energy. You could put it to good use by steering a relationship on the right course. If this means backtracking some steps and having a do-over, so be it. You must learn to go slower.

Friday 17th

A shift of tactics and mood may be more helpful today. You might be more willing to see what went wrong and how you could have avoided this. Fairness and justice in the workplace let you see how sometimes, you have an overwhelming need to act for the greater good.

Saturday 18th

You could have a crisis of conscience today and might beat yourself up about not acting wisely. It may appear that nothing is going your way today. Stay in your shell because coming out might put you at risk of re-opening the wounds you've had recently. Give yourself some thinking space.

Sunday 19th

Your sensitive streak is still visible to all, but if you find
the right connections, it can be soothed. Try not to do any
introspection today as alone, you could make yourself worse.
Connect with your interest groups and reassess your true
north. It's still there, but has your north shifted?

Monday 20th

Stay alert as you could have a revelation of sorts today. It
might be that a light bulb has turned on in your psyche and is
showing you a part of you that was once cherished and then
forgotten. You may wish to resurrect this and look at it in a
new light.

Tuesday 21st

The summer solstice arrives. This is your birthday month.
Happy birthday! Enjoy the longest day with added enthusiasm
in the workplace. This might be the day that your loving
and nurturing nature makes the greatest changes needed.
Conversations with your inner child may also be healing.

Wednesday 22nd

Today you're more driven and passionate about your work.
You could be relentless and vigilant and get a great deal done.
This will be noticed by others and you may gain some brownie
points. Keep doing what you're doing while the energy is there
for you to access.

Thursday 23rd

Venus now enters your private thoughts and will coax you into practising more self-love. You might have some tricky business to deal with, but by evening you may be satisfied that you handled it the best you could. Self-love also means not blaming yourself or thinking you aren't good enough for the job.

Friday 24th

Interest groups can give you the emotional support you need today. They could break things up and put them back together differently for you to see another perspective. This revolutionary way of working might appeal to you now. Get rid of old rubbish by composting it into something new and useful.

Saturday 25th

Be alert for a lesson on boundaries today. As you're emotionally pulled towards a perfect future, you could come across a roadblock. This is Saturn telling you to mind your limits. Your inner compass is also asking you to add healthy boundaries to your core values.

Sunday 26th

Introspection and self-care could be on the agenda today. Take a day to treat and spoil yourself with things you love to do. If your mind doesn't settle on one thing, take that to mean that you have many options and give gratitude for them. Be brave and ask for what you desire.

Monday 27th

Your head and heart are in sync and you begin the week feeling lifted and driven. You may charge headlong into a boundary issue, but you now have some idea how to deal with it. Use your leadership skills and tact to find a workaround solution, but don't attempt to re-invent the wheel.

Tuesday 28th

Neptune turns retrograde today. You could experience this as being a little lost at sea. You will need to scrutinise your inner compass now and see if those things you think you want are truly in alignment with your core values. These might have changed over time.

Wednesday 29th

A new moon in your own sign is a great chance to set big goals and intentions. Think about what you want for yourself. Consider how you appear to the outside world. Your intuition is keen now, so use it wisely. The world is your oyster; be the pearl.

Thursday 30th

You could get your first glimpse of how Neptune retrograde will work for you. A change is needed regarding relationships, but you might need to turn things upside down and look at them differently before you do anything else. Protect your territory and stay safe as you try out a new perspective.

JULY

·················

Friday 1st

This is a particularly good time to ask for what you want.
Finances, pleasure, gratification and home life are the main
themes. Look for quality now. Gather your resources or call
in some debts owed to you. Don't be tempted to settle for less
than you deserve.

Saturday 2nd

You may be challenged by obstacles in your path. These
could be from your outer world but could equally be in your
subconscious. You could be indecisive or simply not speaking
up for yourself, which can lead to feelings of low self-esteem.
Take time to process your thoughts before making them heard.

Sunday 3rd

Consider what belongs solely to you and what you share
with another today. It may be that you're tied or committed
to something which is holding you back. Go through old
documents methodically and see if you can find a loophole.
You may be paying out unnecessarily.

Monday 4th

There is something important which needs completing at
work. You could have a rush of energy to do this, but don't
overdo it. Your productivity could be noticed and approved of
and this could lead to better things for you. Conversations with
your inner critic may hurt you, so don't engage with them.

Tuesday 5th

Today can be exhausting as your social calendar appears to be filling up. You might find that you're in demand in your social groups and some interesting developments are coming. A busy mind will continue for some time as you are learning and communicating new things now.

Wednesday 6th

You could find yourself conflicted with obligations between home and work. This might be a balancing act you will need to equalise before making any big changes. Spend time discussing all your options and make sure that everyone is on the same page. There could be some difficult conversations to be had.

Thursday 7th

Thinking about what you're worth to people could get you into knots. Why not ask them instead? You may be extra sensitive now if your sense of self is tied up with your roles in the family. You may wish to work out why you feel this way.

Friday 8th

Getting creative can help you to work at a pace better suited to you. If you try to keep up with others you could feel drained or unwell. Intense feelings can help you to tease out a behaviour pattern and help you understand why you react in certain ways.

Saturday 9th

Today might be tricky. You could be too emotionally invested to express yourself properly. This could lead to friction and fallouts. A reminder of a similar incident in the past doesn't help and takes you back to a place you dislike. You might be over-sensitive and defensive with friends.

Sunday 10th

If you wake with a feeling of unease, resolve to change it. A day of getting on with your mundane chores could be the distraction you need. You could also have a revelation or two and have more insight into your coping mechanisms. Maybe it's time to try a new way.

Monday 11th

Don't allow self-doubt to be the reason you miss out on something at work. You might feel unworthy or under-qualified. Believe that this is being offered to you for a reason. Grab it with both hands and ensure that you keep informed. This could be too good to miss.

Tuesday 12th

Look at a challenge from the bottom up. You must be strategic now and make a plan of positive small steps. Friends and social groups can be encouraging and supportive. A partner may also offer an ear but could also bring out your shadow side which you project onto them.

Wednesday 13th

There is a full moon in your partner zone today. You might now see that your relationship has reached a different level. Are you content with this? Your mind may still have doubts, or you could become needy and vulnerable. Is this over-sensitivity or does it have any basis in fact?

Thursday 14th

Today you might feel too open and exposed to others. It could be that your desire to go deeper with someone, or with a new subject is opening old wounds. You may need to find your inner compass, get back into alignment and back off from pushing too far.

Friday 15th

It's likely that you've disturbed a wasp's nest and let out a few stingers. Limitations may have been reached, or boundaries have been crossed and resentment is building up. You could experience a lot of friction. A quiet day alone with no contacts is advised while you process this for yourself.

Saturday 16th

Today you must listen and wait for messages to come to you. These could be from your unconscious, gut feelings or symbolic images. You may be more inclined to explore your wider options now. Travel or higher education might be on the agenda. Seek out your friends this evening.

Sunday 17th

A change of perspective may signal an 'aha!' moment for
you today. This can be revolutionary and will need careful
consideration. An act of self-love would be a great activity now,
so do something which lets the love in and fills your soul.
Favourite foods or movies could be just the things.

Monday 18th

Venus drops into your sign and you could become more nurturing
now. You feel more aligned with your inner compass than in recent
days. If a change is needed you can implement it without fear as
you may now see the value in doing your deepest inner work.

Tuesday 19th

Today can be quite exciting and you will need to be alert for
opportunities in the workplace. A new project or responsibility
might be ready for you to jump on board. It's time for you to
put yourself in the spotlight and reap the rewards. Shine your
own light and step into your worth.

Wednesday 20th

Go slowly today and learn all you can about new roles and
responsibilities. This may take some time to assimilate so don't
beat yourself up if you aren't getting it the first time. Laying
the foundations down and making them strong is the most
important task now.

Thursday 21st

Your drive is on fire today, but take care not to get
overwhelmed. You might be assertive and unstoppable, but
this will wear you out if you don't remember to take breaks
and refuel. Remember that you are in the process of putting
down roots and learning something new. Take baby steps.

Friday 22nd

It's possible that you're feeling the effects of trying to run before you can walk. You could be restless and unsure of how to get rid of excess energy. You might cross a boundary with an elder or boss, so be humble. Check in with your true north and realign.

Saturday 23rd

You might wish to take a day all to yourself and put some of your affairs in order. This could simply be a tidy up of your home or a day to switch off and relax. Either way, a day doing what you want will be beneficial and recharge you.

Sunday 24th

Another day of you time would be good. There could be jobs in the home that are outstanding and as your energy is high, these can be completed now. You might also be working from home at your own pace and consolidating things you've learned recently.

Monday 25th

You might not be ready for the working week and could be resentful today. Put your dreams and visions to one side and get on with your duties. Your personal path will still be there when you return home and you can look forward to settling back into your nest this evening.

Tuesday 26th

You could have a brief struggle with work and personal duties today. It might be as simple as double-booking appointments or forgetting about one. However, this evening you may still be in the mood to indulge yourself with good food and company and could overspend on a little luxury.

Wednesday 27th

Today there is excellent energy which will allow you to do something unusual or make a breakthrough with your interest groups. You could find that you are raising issues which can be electrically charged and exhilarating. These might feel good and be in perfect alignment for you, make sure they are sustainable.

Thursday 28th

Jupiter turns retrograde today under a new moon. This is passionate energy and can give you the chance to reassess a recent offer and make sure it's still what you want. Try to keep emotions out of any decision making as this will make it harder if you need to decline.

Friday 29th

You could feel irritable today and in need of some good advice. It might be time to consider what holds worth for you and make decisions based on that. Your self-doubt may be troubling you again. Go within and ask your inner compass for guidance.

Saturday 30th

Although your head and heart are in discussions, you could experience a roadblock or a perceived limitation. Make sure that this isn't in your own mind and you're doing yourself an injustice. Take time to check all the details of something you've been offered. Go through it methodically with legal advice.

Sunday 31st

Watch out today as your frustrations could have you speaking out of turn and saying something you will later regret. There could be a light at the end of the tunnel, but you may need to think outside the box to understand what it requires from you.

AUGUST

· · · · · · · · · · · · · · · · ·

Monday 1st

Today may be explosive in more way than one. The planetary energy is volatile and suggests that you duck out of the way. If it's you throwing things around, like a boomerang, it will come back to you. Best to look after your health today. Take care on the roads.

Tuesday 2nd

Restless energy can propel you into something which needs urgent attention. This could be spending time with your wider social circles. You might be called on to negotiate or restore harmony. Alternatively, this energy can be the motivation you need to do something for yourself. Don't be afraid, just do it.

Wednesday 3rd

You might have reached a state of equilibrium and could be pleased with your performance. Gratitude is owed to you now. You might shun this and do yourself out of the limelight. Modesty is a virtue, but you must accept your part in making something good. Think about this for a while.

Thursday 4th

You may have recently learned a lesson about teamwork or accepting a challenge. This steps up a notch now as you can become more discerning in communicating or extremely proficient in research. You can be more creative or romantic now as your fun side has come out of your shell.

Friday 5th

Something may be bubbling up inside you. What is causing a disturbance now? This might not be negative as it's more likely to be that you have intense feelings towards something from the past. It could initiate a new creative project or an old one may be revisited.

Saturday 6th

Your self-love could be improving and you see signs of that today. Watery energy can make you more sensitive and emotional and maybe a little lost too. This will pass, so go with the flow until you find a landing ground again. However, when you get there you may be tempted to explore.

Sunday 7th

Outgoing energy can take you to new places today. A cheerful outlook can be infectious, and people will want to be around you. You could be looking at things in a new way which will benefit your endeavours. Check your health now as you may have neglected it recently.

Monday 8th

Limits and regulations could put a dampener on your good spirits but can also help you to find another way around. This could be one of those things where you can't jump in at the deep end. You must find the rule book and follow the step by step instructions.

Tuesday 9th

Be careful today as you might find yourself being directed. This can also mean guided, but you will need to recognise this. It might be problematic if you believe that you're being led astray or used in some way.

Wednesday 10th

Partner time can be up and down today. You could feel energised by relating and wish to do sensual or practical things together. This might turn into a need to break free from each other as no-one's needs are being met. Take a break and assess what it is you need in a relationship.

Thursday 11th

You have a strong sense of what is right and fair. If you find yourself in a position of standing up for the underdog, ensure that you aren't putting your career at risk. You could have misread a situation or be getting involved in something which doesn't concern you.

Friday 12th

A full moon occurs and asks that you take a good look at how you are intimate with another. Other planetary energy suggests that today could be challenging and you could clash with people from friendship and interest groups. There's no point pushing issues today, wait for calmer energy.

Saturday 13th

You might have to go into your shell and weather the storm today. There's a possibility that conversations and interactions are muddled and causing tension. You might think you have all the facts, but there may also be something vital which is missing from the whole picture.

Sunday 14th

Your inner compass is available, and you might wish to hold it tightly. It's possible that you're going through changes which are out of your control and you need anchoring. Merging with friends from distant lands can give you some light-hearted distraction without the fear of conflict or judgement. Be open to something fresh.

Monday 15th

Emotions can be bigger than usual today. You might be taking on something at work and feeling overwhelmed. Ask for help. Make all the inquiries you need to get a solid foundation for the work to be done. Don't let your health suffer because of your pride.

Tuesday 16th

Know your limits today as you could be tested. This could be in your intimate relationships or with a teacher or leader in your groups. Listen carefully as you might discover something worth your while. This may be revolutionary and make you sit up and pay attention. A change or ending may be difficult to make.

Wednesday 17th

You could be in the mood for a midweek social activity with friends. However, you may think twice as money could be tight right now. An evening at home doing something you enjoy would also suffice. Good food and company can bring more pleasure than big spends.

Thursday 18th

Inspiration might come your way and you may be keen to try something out. You could also be more compassionate with your work colleagues. Watch that you don't get too stressed today as it's possible you could blow a fuse. Stay away from over-inflated egos and bossy people.

Friday 19th

Pay attention to any dreams you might have; they may be signalling a route you've been reluctant to take. They could also be filling you with illusions. Get grounded today and be practical. Relationships may be going through a change or a review. Friendship groups can distract you from this worry.

Saturday 20th

You could be burning the midnight oil and trying to fit in too much. A busy mind is about to get even busier and more critical. It might feel that you're being inspected and wish to be more protective. It could also be that you're getting somewhere with your personal growth.

Sunday 21st

Any attempt to be scholarly could fail miserably today. Your mind may be too busy or too muddled to concentrate on any one thing. Follow your heart instead and give yourself a day off. Internalising problems won't help either. Do mundane jobs to distract you from bigger things.

Monday 22nd

Self-expression can come across as boasting or desperate. If you have something to say, only do so if it's kind, true and respectful. It could be your head which is on the chopping block. Speaking your mind now will expose your most vulnerable parts and you may not be ready for that.

Tuesday 23rd

This can be a productive day. Applying your mind to tasks can result in some great ideas. Problem-solving activities may suit you best as you are more inclined to think outside the box. Consider shared tasks and teamwork to get things done.

Wednesday 24th

Uranus turns retrograde today. It's possible that you see changes or lack of progress within your social group. A new thing is brewing and will be ready in a few months. You might need to have some good old chatter with a close friend. Put the world to rights and have a laugh today.

Thursday 25th

Check in with people you haven't seen for a while. Old friends or siblings can exchange unconditional love and best wishes. You may need them to cheer you on if you are filling your mind with self-doubt again. Be proactive, not defensive. You're worthy of good things.

Friday 26th

Today can be tricky if once again your self-esteem is low. You could take any comment as criticism. As a Cancer your soft core is delicate, but you might be perceiving things wrongly. Try to take an objective view. If someone is offering advice it can be beneficial to your growth.

Saturday 27th

Your mood may pick up with the arrival of a new moon. This can be the beginning of a new cycle in communication and learning. What goals would you like to set today? Choose wisely as the planetary energy suggests you could overload yourself again.

Sunday 28th

Stay alert as you could find that your caring nature is being taken advantage of today. You may be willing to do something without payment, but this might lead to another favour and before you know it, your day is taken up with things for others. Stand up for yourself and say no if necessary.

Monday 29th

Your head and heart are in sync and you can aim for a healthy balance of activity and home life. It might be possible to talk to your older family members and get a few historical events straight. You could still be thinking of things through the eyes of a child.

Tuesday 30th

A conflict could arise today between home and work. You might be bringing work home which will impact on your time with your tribe. If extra work is imperative, you must ensure that your family understand this, or you could become resentful of both parties.

Wednesday 31st

Call on your mental faculties today and put emotions aside. You might need to problem-solve with someone who has more experience than you. Relationships may still be evolving and morphing. You may need to touch base with this, as intense feelings cause you to worry or stress. Express your needs and concerns to a romantic partner.

SEPTEMBER

· · · · · · · · · · · · · · · · · ·

Thursday 1st

The past may haunt you a little today. Emotional connections remain in your awareness and could be triggered by an event in your wider groups. Alternatively, you could be resurrecting a skill you once used. This is also a good time to dispose of something which no longer serves you.

Friday 2nd

You could face some challenges today from different areas of life. However, they are all centred on one thing. Doubts about your worth may creep in periodically and impact your relationships, work and ability to learn anything intellectual. This is a mindset that you need to alter now.

Saturday 3rd

Your energy could be high this morning but then may fade as the day progresses. Chores and mundane duties need to be done early. Put your mind to outstanding tasks and don't take on anything new as this may drain you. Give yourself some free time to enjoy the weekend. Explore your options.

Sunday 4th

Today you might need to settle something financially or aesthetically in your home. This can bring you some relief or joy and can be an outward expression of your inner self. Try to be flexible and go with the flow this afternoon as being too fixed on something may be frustrating.

Monday 5th

Personal relationships may be rocky today as you navigate family problems. These are minor but could involve a juggling act. You have the skill to communicate and bring things into harmony, but don't allow yourself to be taken for a ride. Stand up for yourself even when helping others.

Tuesday 6th

There is much nicer energy today for you to gently pursue anything regarding your contacts and relationships. Stay alert though as there might be something which isn't quite what it seems. This may be revealed over time and can guide you into an alternate route on your personal path.

Wednesday 7th

Communication is key today. You can be more willing to listen and learn from others. Unusual approaches can be integrated into your family life and restore equilibrium. This evening you might also find that introspection is giving you a newfound passion. You could now be dedicated to healing old wounds.

Thursday 8th

Do the right thing and be a passive observer today. You might spot trouble brewing in your social circles. If it doesn't involve you, be a spectator or stay away. A sense of responsibility doesn't mean that you need to contribute to this. Remember not to blur your personal boundaries.

Friday 9th

Long distance connections can be sweet and fulfilling. You might wish to explore travel options now or find a spirituality which suits your needs. It could be that you're extra dreamy today and ask big questions of the universe. Open your heart and let spirit flow through you.

Saturday 10th

Mercury turns retrograde. Make all the usual preparations. You might notice unfairness or disharmony at home for a short while. A full moon brings out the poet in you and you may start dreaming of exotic places. Watching travel documentaries can be a satisfying activity and allows you to relax this weekend.

Sunday 11th

Eagerness and urgency could be your themes for the day. You might be inspired by something which has moved you. This may mean that you have a bright idea or a big plan you are keen to divulge. Remember that while Mercury is retrograde, new plans are unlikely to be successful.

Monday 12th

You could have a great attitude to begin the working week. Perhaps your new ideas are work-related. You might be passionate about jumping on a good cause for the greater good now, but you will need to assess it fully first. Don't commit to anything just yet.

113

Tuesday 13th

If there's a possibility of rooting one of your plans do it today. Doing the groundwork can make a solid foundation from which little seeds may grow. Your social and interest groups could be a source of inspiration and encouragement. An unusual idea may need teamwork to manifest into the world.

Wednesday 14th

Listen to your intuition today as you could be on to something huge. Quality connections can help to bring out your inner genius. A problem shared may be solved with like-minded people and can be revolutionary. Lead the way and do something spectacular. Take a leap of faith now.

Thursday 15th

You might be reviewing your vision board and checking that what you seek is still in alignment for you. If you need to let something go, honour its place in your life and release it with love. It could be that your needs and wants are evolving into something deeper.

Friday 16th

Take some advice today and slow down. Your big plans might not be ready to be implemented and could fail before they start if you proceed too fast. This evening, you could have some troubling thoughts which may involve your self-worth. Pay no attention and do something practical to ease your mind.

Saturday 17th

You could get yourself in a muddle now as your sensitive soul believes that you don't deserve good things. This might be hard to shake off. It will pass soon, but in the meantime, you may wish to look at old habits or conditioning that have become problems.

Sunday 18th

Don't take things personally today. You could be frustrated at the lack of progress and believe this is a fault of your own. Planetary energy is tricky and can lead you on a downward spiral if you allow it to. Nurture yourself today with good food, good company and things you love to do.

Monday 19th

Challenge yourself to be objective and look at things through different eyes. A period of observation can turn your thoughts around and find the equilibrium you need. Friends and interest groups can be supportive and suggest solutions you may not have thought of before.

Tuesday 20th

The energy is electrically charged but is good for changing things. If you don't wish to do any personal work, you can decide to look at what you have control over and make changes there. This may be as simple as a new look or outfit. Do whatever makes you feel good.

Wednesday 21st

A person in authority might offer their wisdom now. This can be of great value to you later so soak it all up for your consideration. Your motivation may be lacking, but once more this could be an issue with your self-worth. If you need to speak your mind, do so.

Thursday 22nd

Another tricky day can be exhausting if you persist in pushing against the flow. You could be challenged to find a solution to a problem within your friendship groups. Uranus retrograde asks that you assess what is going on here and check if it's still in alignment with your core values.

Friday 23rd

Family life is highlighted now. You must stop, listen and be respectfully responsive to everyone's needs. If the only way to restore harmony is to step back and give each other space, then do this and reconvene when the energy is better suited to working as a unit unconditionally.

Saturday 24th

Conversations must be clear and precise today. There is a tendency to be swept away with illusions or how you think things should be. If something doesn't feel right, it isn't right, Go with your gut now. Serving and helping others must work two ways for a healthy relationship.

Sunday 25th

You might get the emotional support you need today, or you may have found your own strength. Difficult conversations can be made easier when compassion is used. However, you may still wish to keep it low key until Mercury is direct. A new moon can be a peace-keeping influence.

Monday 26th

This is a particularly good day to give yourself a talking to. Find your inner cheerleader and listen to what they say. A small change in intimate relationships can be the first step to getting to know someone or parts of yourself in a more significant way.

Tuesday 27th

Mental energy is high today. Intellectual tasks, problem-solving and deep conversations can fill up your mind space. A tricky conversation with a partner might trigger uneasy feelings and put you on edge. Make sure that you have heard everything correctly and that you are not putting your own biased spin on things.

Wednesday 28th

You could be offering more of yourself and getting very little in return. This might be because you're trying to cross a boundary, and this is disrespectful. If you desire unconditional connections, then you must be prepared to honour all boundaries and accept that some may not be breached.

Thursday 29th

Emotions are high and you could be recalling a past event which had a similar impact on you. Maybe this is holding you back and you should be concentrating on the present. You could be more stubborn than usual and intense jealousy may make you impulsive and defensive.

Friday 30th

Determination and focus can help you regain your senses. You could be dishing out apologies and humbling yourself in order to keep the peace. Make sure that you're sincere in this or you will be found out when you lapse back into your old habits. Make honesty your best policy.

OCTOBER

. . . .

Saturday 1st

The best thing you can do today is to lie low and let everyone else get on with it. If you attempt to do anything bold or make peace, you will fail. The energy suggests that you could be exhausted if you try. Do your own thing and make the most of your weekend.

Sunday 2nd

Don't believe everything you hear today. Mercury turns direct and can cause more confusion with communication. You might think that you're out of the woods, but you're not. Partner time may soothe your soul, but you could also project your unwanted baggage onto someone unsuspecting and cause more problems.

Monday 3rd

Today you might think about romance and friendships. There could be a way to combine both and bring out your creative side too. It's possible that a new romance blossoms out of your social groups. This can give you some pleasant surprises and change the dynamics which have been suffering recently.

Tuesday 4th

Thoughts and emotions can keep you awake. You may be struggling with a change regarding relationships. It could be that you are going through a filtering process and seeing what remains when what you don't want has been discarded. Conversations can be uniquely balanced which may seem like a novelty.

Wednesday 5th

Innovative connections can bring some much-needed lightness to your soul. If you exercise strong boundaries you might find a new passion or relationship which is on a completely new level. You may need to get used to this and learn to connect from your mind and not just your emotions.

Thursday 6th

Today can be very dreamy and you might feel as if you've been whisked away to a fantasy island. Spiritual growth is occurring and it may feel fresh and new. Allow yourself to drift and imagine. Your mind and emotions can meet in the middle.

Friday 7th

Whilst floating on your cloud you may hear your inner voice telling you that what you thought was your mission has been aborted. Navigate towards what your inner compass is telling you now. This may be addictive, and you should try to keep at least one foot on the ground.

Saturday 8th

You might have a lot to think about today. Your inner compass is available, and you should check in. Retain an open heart today and allow new thoughts and feelings to flow. This afternoon you may begin to see the journey ahead and plan accordingly. Just don't weigh yourself down again.

Sunday 9th

Pluto turns direct and has finished rearranging relationships. It's up to you to deal with the fallout. A full moon is an excellent time to look back at how far you've come since spring. Pare away anything that might be impeding further progress or slowing you down.

Monday 10th

Your energy is high today and you can be extra productive. Gather more facts and do some last-minute research on a project which you're about to be heavily involved in. You could be grieving for something you've let go of recently. It's okay to honour what it once meant to you.

Tuesday 11th

Your family life could become filled with chatter now. There may be negotiations to be made or family conferences regarding fairness and equality. Legal issues are possible, and you may need to hire a professional. You could also be studying something which brings balance to your home and work lives.

Wednesday 12th

Be mindful of how you communicate today in the workplace. You could encounter a big stop sign and will need to think outside the box to resolve this. Stubborn energy prevents you from moving on so take this time to find a different perspective or remove unattainable and unrealistic goals.

Thursday 13th

Introspection would do you good today. Go within yourself and look at your habitual reactions. Have you outgrown them, or do you still cling on to them because they once helped? It may be time to adapt to a more mature and evolved way of reacting to outside stimuli and triggers.

Friday 14th

Air energy can make your mind exceptionally busy today. Searching your psyche for pearls of wisdom may result in several 'aha!' moments. Revelations stack up and you might kick yourself for not having seen these before. Be good to yourself and learn where your boundaries have been blurred.

Saturday 15th

The early hours may bring vivid dreams and you wake needing to sort fact from fiction. Is it a memory or a dream that has been triggering vulnerable feelings within you? You may need help to answer this question and your family of birth may provide the answers. Nurture your inner child.

Sunday 16th

Today you can be protective or defensive of your own environment. If you need to stay in your shell and take a day off, gather nourishing resources and feed your soul with things you love to do. Nobody will blame you for having a day of quality time to yourself.

Monday 17th

Starting the working week may seem like a burden as you could still be feeling vulnerable and may not wish to be exposed. Your inner compass doesn't seem to be working and you may feel lost. Under this influence, you may feel attacked or manipulated. Watch out for passive-aggressive behaviour.

. . . .

Tuesday 18th

Your voice returns and you could be feeling stronger today.
Keep your inner fire burning and stand up for yourself. Self-
expression in the workplace could go two ways, so ensure that
what you need to say is true, respectful and kind. You could
use defensiveness or self-righteousness to cope.

Wednesday 19th

It's possible that you're at the other end of the scale since the
weekend. You could be brash and obnoxious in order to cover
up your perceived weaknesses. People will see through this
as it isn't the real you. Watch out for clashes with your social
groups. Especially the leaders.

Thursday 20th

A change of mood and energy might bring you back to your
normal self. It could be that a friend or family member has
reminded you who you are and that you are cherished for
being authentic. You could feel silly for being stroppy or
childish when wanting your own way.

Friday 21st

An energetically quiet day may allow you to come back to your
centre and ground yourself. Practical activities which need
thorough mental processes would be good for you. Filing,
sorting, administration or decluttering will help take your
mind off any recent worries and lift your self-esteem. Keep
yourself occupied this way.

Saturday 22nd

Stay away from dreaming or attempting to find your inner compass. Today is needed for essential maintenance of your body. Make a medical appointment if you've been neglecting your health recently. You may need a tonic, but for now, a walk in nature or physical exercise will suffice.

Sunday 23rd

Saturn turns direct today and will ease some of the pressure in your intimate relationships. You might have learned some valuable lessons about boundaries this year. The next few weeks are about to get creative and seductive, so you may wish to practice maintaining healthy boundaries even more now.

Monday 24th

Your head and heart are in sync and you might feel much more balanced. Your rational and logical side matches your emotions and brings a sense of calm. A fresh new perspective on relating to deep levels can be exciting and you are eager to explore what this means for you.

Tuesday 25th

A new moon and a solar eclipse open a window of wild card energy. This can be intimate and exotic, and you may need to keep your wits about you. As Venus is also involved, this will almost certainly involve romance or creative projects. Stay grounded as you could fall madly in love.

Wednesday 26th

A shock or a ghost from the past could visit and you will need to deal with it once and for all. Be firm but fair and throw the past back to where it belongs. This may be your first chance to exercise a strong boundary and say no.

Thursday 27th

Stay alert and be mindful that you could be prone to illusions now. You could be charmed into believing that a euphoric state is the real thing when it may just be a lovely drug. Get out and do your mundane duties and take your mind off romance for now.

Friday 28th

Your sense of joy and optimism could be disguised as something else right now. If you experience a big pull into spiritual enlightenment, stay safe as this could also be an illusion. Travel and the exotic attract you now, but are not really options. Be satisfied with documentaries and research.

Saturday 29th

It's possible that you've been knocked off course and could be asking for a lifeboat to get back to shore. You may have bitten off more than you can chew. Be humble and ask for the help you need to re-orient yourself. A trusted friend or partner can help.

Sunday 30th

Mars turns retrograde now. This will occur in your most private thoughts and you may have a period of slowing down your internal progress. Use it as a rest stop and enjoy the break. Partner time can be sensual and delightful without all the high romance, music and poetry.

Monday 31st

If you need a little help staying in control and grounded, look to a partner. You might find that they are happy to help if it means they have you on planet Earth for a while. Enjoy a time of shared visions and discuss how the two of you can change the world together.

NOVEMBER

....

Tuesday 1st

Challenges persist and you could be too scared to make a move for fear of disrupting the status quo. The best thing you can do today is to accept and understand your responsibilities towards groups. Change and progress are being made with or without your contribution.

Wednesday 2nd

Go within and find an anchor as you might feel out of your depth today. Just be sure that this isn't an addiction or coping mechanism which is unhealthy. A matter regarding love and romance may need to be dealt with. Is this a ghost from the past that needs banishing?

Thursday 3rd

Fluid energy can make you adaptable to any circumstance but can also feel ungrounded. The emotional realm is where you work naturally, but this may be an overload. It can be consuming but may also help you move things along and work with the changing currents.

Friday 4th

Your inner compass calls and you have a chance to evaluate recent events. You might change your perspective or decide that something is not in alignment with your core values. Emotions may be bigger than usual, so hold tight and accept this journey as it could be the healing you need.

Saturday 5th

It's important that you let go of things which you're using as an emotional crutch. Learn to see yourself as worthy of good things and let unhealthy habits or behaviours go. This may cause you some inner conflict or problems in your romance, but this is necessary for growth.

Sunday 6th

Be proactive today and make lists of things that can help you at work and also with your inner process. A group of like-minded friends could provide what you need to know now. Difficult conversations are the catalyst for discarding anything that is weighing you down or keeping you from moving on.

Monday 7th

Look for quality now. If you've made space in your life, there's room for something new to come in. Don't pick up the first thing you see. Be discerning and only accept what is offered if it has meaning and can bring you pleasure. Choose something you can treasure.

Tuesday 8th

You might feel a pull towards a bright future which has solid roots. A full moon and lunar eclipse close the wild card window of energy. You may feel this strongly and should be passive and let it play out. It could be that something has been removed from your life forever.

Wednesday 9th

Clear up any debris from recent events. You might hear or speak harsh words today and this could upset you. A new cycle is starting and is activated by energy which penetrates and destroys. There is a creative way you can use this energy and you will work this out soon.

Thursday 10th

The gossip line could be busy today as people catch up and make their own versions of events. Ensure you're not the one spreading it. Allow yourself to settle into something creative which is in line with your personal path. This may be dreamy and poetic.

Friday 11th

You could experience a mental block, and this could irritate you. Words escape you or are chosen badly and may result in a misunderstanding. You might perceive this as unfair on your part and try rectifying the problem, but you may not get far. Wait until this energy passes.

Saturday 12th

Your ruler, the moon, drops into your sign and you might notice this by an increase in intuition or sensitivity. Your hopes, dreams and romantic pursuits can be easily communicated now. It could be that you've found a muse or been beguiled by beauty. If you can express it, do so.

Sunday 13th

The earth could shake a little as you feel disturbances around you. These may be exciting and fill you with nervous pleasure. Think of it like a small child waiting for Christmas. You could be on the edge of having everything you've ever wanted. Anticipation is adrenalin for your inner child.

Monday 14th

Seductive energy continues to thrill and fascinate. You could be nourished and soul-fed by romantic and creative activity. Step into your strength and show the world who you are. If you feel like royalty, enjoy the uplift this gives you and notice how much taller you feel.

Tuesday 15th

You could be walking around in a surreal fantasy land. However, you might also be acutely aware and afraid that this could disappear at any moment. A last minute or rushed attempt to enhance your romantic relationships isn't needed. Have confidence that this energy is floating around you for a reason you are yet to understand.

Wednesday 16th

Today you should try to communicate or create something deep and mysterious. This may be uncomfortable for you, but will be the only way you can bring forth what it is you desire. Take a leap of faith and stay true to yourself. Speak without fear.

Thursday 17th

You could be worrying that you've spoken out of turn. Your fear of rejection has you going through everything you've spoken. Don't analyse this too much as you will find yourself in a muddle. Be open-hearted and offer yourself unconditionally. Trust that you're in the right place at the right time.

Friday 18th

Do something which helps you stay grounded today. Practical or mundane activities can be useful to distract you from your internal worries. This evening you might need to put in extra effort as you could be at risk of wallowing in your own lack of confidence.

Saturday 19th

Your home and family can be the support structure you need right now. There's no need to spill everything that's in your mind or heart, just appreciate that they're there for you. Gentle care and lighthearted conversation can be a tonic and make you feel nurtured. They may also give you courage.

Sunday 20th

Knowing your duties and responsibilities today can be a source of harmony. The world still revolves around natural rhythms and cycles, even though you may feel out of balance. Enjoy family time which can be respectful and soothing to your soul. Your contribution will be valued and appreciated.

Monday 21st

Mark this day as extremely auspicious. You could see everything drop into place nicely and could wonder why you worried so much. Important conversations this evening can touch a deep part of you and inspire you to be brave and bold. Go after what you desire with a passionate heart.

Tuesday 22nd

The cosmic waste bin is waiting for you to drop your unhelpful emotional responses in. You may be reviewing how you've experienced sharing in the past. It could be time to think about your security and make plans to try something new. Take your time as letting go is never easy.

Wednesday 23rd

Today you could be successful and take control in relationship matters. This might mean making changes which can be beneficial and life-changing. The intensity of this can be exhilarating and daunting, but if shared with another, it can also connect the two of you on a deeper level than you can imagine.

Thursday 24th

There is wonderful energy for you to access today. A new moon heralds the start of a brave new journey of unconditional love and duty to another. Jupiter turns direct and will bring bounty to your career. Conversations are easy and love is harmonious and heartfelt.

Friday 25th

You could experience a little setback today, but this will soon pass. This might be from within and may be that voice of self-doubt. It could be that you believe you aren't worthy of good things or that you are swimming out of your depth. Don't jump in at the deep end.

Saturday 26th

An easy weekend awaits you. You might contemplate the past and future together and look at where you're standing now. Sharing, caring, finances and pleasure could all be the issues you think about. What didn't work for you in the past may now have a chance of succeeding.

Sunday 27th

Partner time can bring unexpected delight today. You might notice that your dreams are now founded on Earth, which can sustain you better. Change no longer frightens you. The future looks bright and you can look forward to expanding your world vision. Perhaps a course of study or travel is on the agenda.

Monday 28th

An outgoing mood can make people stop and wonder what has happened to you. Don't let anyone bring you down today, not that they could. You don't need to be supercharged and running around because your good spirits are what is motivating you. Your boundaries are strong and healthy.

Tuesday 29th

Thought processes might be doing overtime today. There may be long-standing problems which you are now slowly figuring out. Digging deep and taking time to understand what you find may be the best way to uncover the gold hidden in your psyche. Seek to learn and share your wisdom.

Wednesday 30th

Floaty energy surrounds you once more. You could have a spiritual epiphany which shows you how far you can go and still feel at home. Conversations can be more intellectual or explorative. It's possible that you have found a teacher or guru to guide you on the next part of your journey.

DECEMBER

. . . .

Thursday 1st

Keep a level head today as you might come back down to Earth with a bump. This is a temporary mood, so refrain from making decisions until you have more clarity of vision. You can connect with your inner compass but may need a day alone to process feelings.

Friday 2nd

Try not to talk yourself into, or out of something now. Your emotions could be off the scale but can also be the impetus for making a jump into the unknown. However, don't be too impulsive or impatient. Return to career projects and make lists and plans.

Saturday 3rd

Gathering resources will show your leadership skills in a good light. Those in charge may be impressed by what they see of you today so stick to your duties. You may also show these qualities in your home life and claim your authority as a good administrator.

Sunday 4th

Neptune turns direct today. From your inner compass, you may now have a better direction on where your future lies. What is no longer important to you will dissolve or fade away. You might experience this as a new perspective on an old situation. Plant seeds which have more value to you now.

Monday 5th

Friendship groups could have something new for you today.
There may be a lot of activity with innovative plans going on.
If you want to get involved, you must contribute in some way
which will ensure your part in the team. Quality interactions
can lead to positive action.

Tuesday 6th

You may be in a rush to get a chore done today. Deadlines
could be close and needing your attention. Put your nose
to the grindstone and aim to complete things today. Deep
conversations with a partner are possible and can help you
understand a concept that has been evading you.

Wednesday 7th

Today you have a chance to work at your own pace. This might
be easier for you if unencumbered by outside obligations.
Working alone in an environment free of chatter will help you
focus on the job. Alternatively, you may choose to use today to
review your inner work and progress so far.

Thursday 8th

A full moon may bring you a revelation. Look within yourself
to see what has changed for you this year. You may not have
noticed how much you've grown but the results are there.
Understand that you alone are responsible for changing things
which no longer serve you.

Friday 9th

If you need more time today, ask for it. You could be feeling vulnerable or defensive if people are rushing you. Try to be flexible and stay positive. Don't worry about what others think of you if you need to progress in baby steps or ask a lot of questions.

Saturday 10th

Your relationship zone is blessed with the arrival of Venus. Expect to give and receive more compassion. You might wish to take things slowly and enjoy the journey rather than rush to the next level. Expect the unexpected and go out for some fun with friends to kick off the festive season.

Sunday 11th

You could have vivid dreams and wake thinking about how a partner sees you now. An awareness of the steps you've taken together may overwhelm you until you get a chance to discuss this. Speak your truth and let them know if you have financial concerns.

Monday 12th

The working week begins with putting your heart into your work. You might find more pleasure from doing a job well, even if it takes you longer than expected. Walk tall and be proud that you've given it your best shot. Take time to observe your own work and reward yourself.

Tuesday 13th

Today may be tricky as you may need to push someone's boundaries to get them moving. This isn't meant to hurt them, but it can go against all you've learned this year and it hurts you. Your fast-flowing energy is needed to encourage others to do the same and be productive.

Wednesday 14th

Ground yourself today and get on with practical tasks which are engaging and time-consuming. There's no time for dreaming or idle chatter now. Any conversations can be productive and significant. You may need to ensure that you read all the details and know how something works to understand it.

Thursday 15th

Close partnerships can feel the benefit of grounding energy today. A partner may bring out the best in you and help you be more practical and less emotional. They can ensure that your personal growth is being nurtured and nourished properly and this feeds your Cancerian soul.

Friday 16th

Hopes and dreams need to take a back seat today. You might feel resentful about this as your heart yearns to merge or connect with the ethereal energy you've enjoyed recently. There's work to be done and you need to be thorough. Perhaps you could do a physical end-of-year clear out.

Saturday 17th

To be fair to all, you might need to divide your time between lovers and family. This could tug on the heartstrings a little as you feel you may be letting someone down. A social gathering can be interesting this evening if you have time in your busy social calendar.

Sunday 18th

Today you could have a better idea of how to spend your free time. Prioritising your obligations must come first and then you can leave time to play or relax. You may be pleased with yourself by the end of the day, so treat yourself to something very special.

Monday 19th

The energy is intense now and you must get creative with it. Romantic partners may pull you close and demand more of your attention. This isn't a bad thing unless you lose yourself in the process. Ensure that mind games are not being played as this can hurt your sensitive soul.

Tuesday 20th

High energy can make the air around you electric. This can be volatile or sexy, but either way, you may feel the earth move. You could be putting your foot down and making your own demands as you feel you're being used or manipulated. End anything which is hurting you.

Wednesday 21st

You might have a multitude of chores to do today, but speed and motivation are with you. Perhaps you have deadlines to meet. The winter solstice arrives, and the shortest day gives you added urgency to get things done. Prepare for some cosy time with a partner over the next month.

Thursday 22nd

Love and friendships can bring early surprises today. Stay flexible and be open to invitations. Your diligence when doing mundane tasks meet the approval of elders, but don't overstretch yourself and commit to something which might not be in your best interests. Keep your mind fresh for your own plans.

Friday 23rd

A new moon occurs in your relationship zone and heralds a brand-new start. A project or long-term plan you share with another may seem like hard work but will prove beneficial to you both. This can put a new spin on your relationship or elevate it to another level.

Saturday 24th

Today is filled with anticipation and easy connections. Partner time is highlighted and can be dreamy and loving. You may already feel the effects of a new cycle and look forward to becoming your best self with your dearest. Your intuition tells you that your softness and sensitivity are a bonus.

Sunday 25th

If everything has been prepared, you can enjoy a day of kindness and surprises. This festive day has great planetary energy and you may feel part of something bigger which excites you. Merging and connecting with family and tribe can make you realise how blessed you are.

Monday 26th

It's possible that you're tired and might struggle to fulfil duties today. An event with your social groups may not be as attractive, and declining could be your best option. You might have a good sense of your own limits and save your energy for smaller events closer to home.

Tuesday 27th

Switch off, kick back and do your own thing today. Simply enjoy things which can help you unwind and forget any worries. You may be thinking about holidays or educating yourself about other cultures. Use your free time to research new possibilities. Drift off into your personal fantasy land. No-one will mind.

Wednesday 28th

Nicely timed, your inner compass appears, and you check in with yourself. You may be reminiscing about the year gone by. Gratitude and satisfaction fill your heart as you feel perfectly aligned with who you are and who you now want to become. This is growth and you're doing fine.

Thursday 29th

Mercury turns retrograde today. As always, ensure your communications are clear and double-check travel plans. Your heart may be bursting with ideas you would like to put in place in the coming year. Test these out by having discussions with your partner or closest friend.

Friday 30th

You could be swimming against the tide today and feeling a little irritated. Nothing can progress in the holiday season. Don't allow yourself to get into a bad mood just because you want something instantly and it isn't available or possible. Wait this out with grace and patience.

Saturday 31st

Although the daytime could be challenging, try not to cause friction with a partner. There might be an invitation to celebrate with friends this evening and you could enjoy this. Alternatively, a night alone with a partner may see subtle power games going on. Choose wisely.

Cancer

....

PEOPLE WHO SHARE
YOUR SIGN

PEOPLE WHO
SHARE YOUR SIGN

. . . .

The nurturing influence of Cancer makes this sign the go-to guardian of the zodiac calendar. Teamed with their pioneering instinct, Cancerians have been, and still are, some of the most powerfully empathetic figures in the world, from Nelson Mandela to Malala Yousafzai. The emotional impression that Crabs make is notable, the words of Nobel Prize-winning writers Pablo Neruda and Ernest Hemingway being just two examples. Discover the Cancerians who share your exact birthday and see if you can spot the similarities.

22nd June

Donald Faison (1974), Carson Daly (1973), Dan Brown (1964), Erin Brockovich (1960), Cyndi Lauper (1953), Meryl Streep (1949), Elizabeth Warren (1949), Kris Kristofferson (1936)

23rd June

Melissa Rauch (1980), Jason Mraz (1977), Zinedine Zidane (1972), Selma Blair (1972), Frances McDormand (1957), Randy Jackson (1956), Clarence Thomas (1948), Alan Turing (1912), Anna Akhmatova (1889)

24th June

Candice Patton (1988), Lionel Messi (1987), Solange Knowles (1986), Vanessa Ray (1981), Mindy Kaling (1979), Robert Reich (1946), Robert Downey Sr. (1936), Chuck Taylor (1901)

25th June

Lele Pons (1996), Sheridan Smith (1981), Busy Philipps (1979), Linda Cardellini (1975), George Michael (1963), Ricky Gervais (1961), Anthony Bourdain (1956), Carly Simon (1945), George Orwell (1903), Antoni Gaudí (1852)

26th June

Ariana Grande (1993), King Bach (1988), Aubrey Plaza (1984), Jason Schwartzman (1980), Paul Thomas Anderson (1970), Sean Hayes (1970), Mikhail Khodorkovsky (1963), Chris Isaak (1956)

27th June

Lauren Jauregui (1996), Matthew Lewis (1989), Ed Westwick (1987), Sam Claflin (1986), Khloé Kardashian (1984), Tobey Maguire (1975), Vera Wang (1949), Helen Keller (1880)

28th June

Kevin De Bruyne (1991), Markiplier (1989), Tamara Ecclestone (1984), Rob Dyrdek (1974), Elon Musk (1971), John Cusack (1966), Kathy Bates (1948), Mel Brooks (1926)

29th June

Kawhi Leonard (1991), Éver Banega (1988), Nicole Scherzinger (1978), Charlamagne tha God (1978), Marcus Wareing (1970), Melora Hardin (1967), Gary Busey (1944), Antoine de Saint-Exupéry (1900)

30th June

Michael Phelps (1985), Cheryl Tweedy (1983), Katherine Ryan (1983), Lizzy Caplan (1982), James Martin (1972), Phil Anselmo (1968), Vincent D'Onofrio (1959), Lena Horne (1917)

. . . .

1st July

Léa Seydoux (1985), Liv Tyler (1977), Missy Elliott (1971), Pamela Anderson (1967), Diana, Princess of Wales (1961), Dan Aykroyd (1952), Debbie Harry (1945), Olivia de Havilland (1916)

2nd July

Margot Robbie (1990), Alex Morgan (1989), Lindsay Lohan (1986), Ashley Tisdale (1985), Peter Kay (1973), Jerry Hall (1956), Larry David (1947), Hermann Hesse (1877)

3rd July

Sebastian Vettel (1987), Olivia Munn (1980), Patrick Wilson (1973), Tom Cruise (1962), Faye Resnick (1957), Gloria Allred (1941), Franz Kafka (1883)

4th July

Malia Ann Obama (1998), Post Malone (1995), Mike Sorrentino (1982), Elie Saab (1964), Calvin Coolidge, U.S. President (1872), Giuseppe Garibaldi (1807), Nathaniel Hawthorne (1804)

5th July

Dejan Lovren (1989), Tess Holliday (1985), Megan Rapinoe (1985), Pauly D (1980), Amélie Mauresmo (1979), Susan Wojcicki (1968), Claudia Wells (1966), Edie Falco (1963), Paul Smith (1946)

6th July

Eva Green (1980), Kevin Hart (1979), 50 Cent (1975), Jennifer Saunders (1958), George W. Bush, U.S. President (1946), Sylvester Stallone (1946), Tenzin Gyatso, 14th Dalai Lama (1935), Nancy Reagan (1921), Frida Kahlo (1907), Marc Chagall (1887)

7th July

Ashton Irwin (1994), Ally Brooke (1993), Jack Whitehall (1988), MS Dhoni (1981), Kirsten Vangsness (1972), Jim Gaffigan (1966), Jeremy Kyle (1965), Shelley Duvall (1949), Ringo Starr (1940)

8th July

Jaden Smith (1998), Son Heung-min (1992), Jake McDorman (1986), Sophia Bush (1982), Milo Ventimiglia (1977), Kevin Bacon (1958), Anjelica Huston (1951), John D. Rockefeller (1839)

9th July

Douglas Booth (1992), Amanda Knox (1987), Jack White (1975), Courtney Love (1964), Jordan Belfort (1962), Kelly McGillis (1957), Tom Hanks (1956), Lindsey Graham (1955)

10th July

Isabela Moner (2001), Perrie Edwards (1993), Golshifteh Farahani (1983), Jessica Simpson (1980), Adrian Grenier (1976), Sofía Vergara (1972), Urban Meyer (1964), Marcel Proust (1871)

11th July

Alessia Cara (1996), Caroline Wozniacki (1990), Justin Chambers (1970), Lisa Rinna (1963), Richie Sambora (1959), Sela Ward (1956), Giorgio Armani (1934), Yul Brynner (1920)

12th July

Malala Yousafzai (1997), James Rodríguez (1991), Phoebe Tonkin (1989), Topher Grace (1978), Michelle Rodriguez (1978), Anna Friel (1976), Sundar Pichai (1972), Cheryl Ladd (1951), Richard Simmons (1948), Pablo Neruda (1904)

13th July

Rich the Kid (1992), Leon Bridges (1989), Tulisa (1988), Ken Jeong (1969), Cheech Marin (1946), Ernő Rubik (1944), Harrison Ford (1942), Patrick Stewart (1940), Simone Veil (1927)

14th July

Conor McGregor (1988), Victoria, Crown Princess of Sweden (1977), David Mitchell (1974), Matthew Fox (1966), Jane Lynch (1960), Bebe Buell (1953), Gerald Ford, U.S. President (1913), Gustav Klimt (1862)

15th July

Damian Lillard (1990), Travis Fimmel (1979), Gabriel Iglesias (1976), Diane Kruger (1976), Brian Austin Green (1973), Brigitte Nielsen (1963), Forest Whitaker (1961), Linda Ronstadt (1946)

16th July

Luke Hemmings (1996), Gareth Bale (1989), AnnaLynne McCord (1987), Jayma Mays (1979), Corey Feldman (1971), Will Ferrell (1967), Phoebe Cates (1963), Ginger Rogers (1911), Ida B. Wells (1862)

17th July

Billie Lourd (1992), Tom Fletcher (1985), Gino D'Acampo (1976), Gavin McInnes (1970), Jason Clarke (1969), Angela Merkel, German Chancellor (1954), David Hasselhoff (1952), Camilla, Duchess of Cornwall (1947), Donald Sutherland (1935)

18th July

Priyanka Chopra (1982), Michiel Huisman (1981), Kristen Bell (1980), Stefan Janoski (1979), Kelly Reilly (1977), M.I.A. (1975), Vin Diesel (1967), Richard Branson (1950), Hunter S. Thompson (1937), John Glenn (1921), Nelson Mandela (1918)

19th July

Shane Dawson (1988), Jared Padalecki (1982), Benedict Cumberbatch (1976), Nicola Sturgeon (1970), Brian May (1947), Vladimir Mayakovsky (1893), Edgar Degas (1834)

20th July

Ben Simmons (1996), Alycia Debnam-Carey (1993), Julianne Hough (1988), Gisele Bündchen (1980), Sandra Oh (1971), Anton du Beke (1966), Chris Cornell (1964), Natalie Wood (1938)

21st July

Maggie Lindemann (1998), Juno Temple (1989), Paloma Faith (1981), Josh Hartnett (1978), Ross Kemp (1964), Robin Williams (1951), Cat Stevens (1948), Ernest Hemingway (1899)

22nd July

Prince George of Cambridge (2013), Selena Gomez (1992), Keegan Allen (1989), John Leguizamo (1964), David Spade (1964), Willem Dafoe (1955), Don Henley (1947), Danny Glover (1946), Oscar de la Renta (1932), Bob Dole (1923)